The Four Types of Wealth

What Types of Wealth Are You Building? Redesign Your Lifestyle and Improve Your Work-Life Balance

Mark Davies

Uranus Publishing

Contents

INTRODUCTION

In today's world, an increasing number of people prefer the tangible content of their lives to the immaterial content of their money accounts. In summary, how you spend your money today matters more than how wealthy you are. The doctrine of "living large with your money after retirement" is dead. The ultimate 21st-century desire, on the other hand, is to live on your own terms.

People's imaginations have been captivated for years by the notion that children will have a better life than their parents due to economic prosperity. Young people should work hard for diplomas, get a respectable profession, and buy a house, and they will eventually be better off than their parents owing to the economy.

This theory is no longer a given in the twenty-first century.

Many variables, including an unknowable employment market, urbanization, globalization, and technological innovation, have influenced millennials' perceptions of wealth and money. As a result, many people are turning away from the traditional path to wealth in favor of a new lifestyle.

Please, don't misunderstand me. Being financially wealthy is still a very common dream. Most people, however, don't want to be a millionaire because they enjoy gazing at the numbers on their bank statement. They simply yearn for a millionaire's lifestyle.

Tim Ferriss' 4-Hour Workweek, published in 2007, transformed money, work, and lifestyle design concepts. Some of the book's lessons and techniques are now out of date, but its essential principles remain relevant. The concept of lifestyle design is one of these guiding ideas. It is, in my opinion, the "ability to live the way you choose with sufficient money, health, leisure, and the correct environment." Tim emphasizes in this context that enjoying your ideal lifestyle does not rely entirely on your financial wealth. It is determined by how, when, and where you use your resources.

Money may solve a lot of difficulties and provide mental freedom. However, if your financial wealth is related to a lack of time, fulfillment, and purpose, it will not improve your life. Therefore, attempting to become rich on paper is a futile endeavor. A perfectly designed lifestyle, on the other hand, is a goal that deserves all our efforts.

Money should be used to increase the quality of your life, not as an end goal. Starting from this assumption, I decided to write this book to convey all my knowledge on the subject in an organized manner.

Personally, I reached the conviction that time is the new form of wealth years ago, after working for years in the financial sector. My life was gratifying professionally and financially, and I certainly couldn't complain from that standpoint. As time went by, I realized that that success at work came at an increasing price. I was giving up all the things I had always enjoyed and had less time to spend with the people I love. I had more money, but I had less time.

After much reflection, I then decided to make a radical change. I stopped following a pattern of life that I had not chosen but only passively followed. In my workshops, I describe the method thoroughly to follow my path to financial independence and early retirement.

In this book, instead, I will address the topic of financial freedom from the lifestyle perspective. We will take an in-depth look at the differences between the various types of wealth, how to achieve them, and how to maintain them.

In redesigning our lifestyle, we will also open a window on the possibility of changing the place where we live, always with the aim of balancing the four forms of wealth.

We'll discover together how you can increase your income, reduce your expenses, and save the money you need for investments. If pursued and implemented with commitment, this strategy will lead us to financial freedom, which is the prerequisite to stop exchanging our time for money.

Only at that point, our true wealth will be time.

We will be able to occupy it as we prefer, in the place we like and with the people we love most.

This will be a multifaceted but challenging journey.

Let's get started!

Chapter One

THE FOUR TYPES OF WEALTH

I n 2018, James Clear, the best-selling author of Atomic Habits, tweeted the following about different forms of wealth:

- Financial wealth (money)
- Social wealth (status)
- Time wealth (freedom)
- Physical wealth (health)

I like this list, for it concisely broadens the idea of wealth beyond money and financial possessions. Since, just as I feel there is a danger in equating being rich with being wealthy, I also believe there is a danger in operating on the assumption that there is just one form of wealth, and that it is monetary.

Most people instinctively associate the term "wealth" with an abundance of money. However, this is a limiting definition of being affluent. Wealth encompasses all aspects of one's life, including health, relationships, finances, time, and so on.

According to research, families who have maintained wealth for more than three generations frequently have different perspectives and definitions of wealth. These wealthy families view prosperity from different angles, money being only one of them.

Many cultures have the adage "shirtsleeves to shirtsleeves in three generations." It effectively expresses the idea that money earned by one generation is rarely passed down to the next two generations. That happens because many families frequently fail to recognize the relevance of non-monetary wealth in long-term sustainability.

Money is a vital instrument in successful multigenerational families, but it is not the only one. They should also emphasize recognizing and fostering other forms of wealth, such as one's self (human capital), relationships (social capital), and values (cultural capital). This advancement is essential to the successful transmission of wealth from generation to generation.

Balancing different types of wealth

When it comes to the four categories of wealth, there is a big trap that most people fall into and cannot escape.

Here's the catch: Be aware of employment that offers financial wealth (money) and social wealth (status) but deprives you of time wealth (freedom), and physical wealth (health).

This is the primary issue that the modern world faces, and it is vital to know that you can unknowingly fall into this misunderstanding if you do not actively pursue what is meaningful and wise on your life's journey.

Most people prioritize money and status over freedom and health. In the short term, this "works" slightly in the individual's favor, but in the long run, it has negative implications. Someone can attain financial and social wealth while feeling as if they are on the right track, but if they do not care for their time and physical wealth, they are subconsciously going down the road to self-destruction.

What good is having all the money and status in the world if you don't have time to enjoy yourself or the physical vitality to feel good? The response is that there is no benefit to that compromise.

And it is a tradeoff, though it is frequently made unconsciously rather than consciously.

To gain a better knowledge of your current situation and whether you are trapped in your life, ask yourself the following questions:

- "Do I recognize the benefit in prioritizing my time and health, in addition to my wealth and status, and does it show in my actions?"
- "In which of the four forms of wealth am I lacking, and how can I improve immediately?"
- "In which of the four categories of riches do I excel?"

What type of wealth are you building?

We all have the opportunity to reach all four types of riches in our life, and when we do, an odd thing happens: we begin to feel the richness of fulfillment. The wealth of fulfillment is achieved when all four categories of riches interact and are constantly improved upon. This is where we'd all like to be.

Keep in mind that each of these sorts of riches takes years to master and, in some ways, might be viewed as a life-long process that never ends because these sorts of money have no destination. There is only ever-increasing progress.

What type of wealth are you trying to build?

Each of these forms of wealth takes years of effort, practice, humility, learning, understanding, networking, etc., to perfect, so forget about the myth that says you can't work on all of them simultaneously and get started right away!

In the following chapters, we'll go through each of these four types of wealth in detail to give you a better understanding of how they connect to your personal life.

Chapter Two

FINANCIAL WEALTH

F inancial wealth is the amount of money or assets that a person has accumulated. It is the most visible sort of wealth, and what the majority of people in our society strive for. The pressure to accumulate financial riches is ubiquitous, which in turn can harm your ability to achieve other sorts of wealth.

But what exactly does financial wealth imply? Financial wealth, I believe, is financial freedom; it is the opportunity to spend money on what you want, when you want, and with whomever you want. In other words, financial freedom means complete independence from financial instability and worries, which are great sources of sorrow in most people's lives.

Understanding and mastering the following fundamentals will lead to financial wealth.

Investing (Assets vs. Liabilities)

In his famous book "Rich Dad, Poor Dad," Robert Kiyosaki says, "You must know the difference between an asset and a liability, and buy assets.... Rich people acquire assets. Poor and middle-class people acquire liabilities, but they think they are assets."

This is such a basic and crucial rule that far too many people overlook, so let's start with the basics.

We keep score in the game of accumulating money by using a balance sheet. Consider a balance sheet to be nothing more than a sheet of paper with a vertical line down the middle. A list of assets appears on the balance sheet's left side. A list of liabilities appears on the right side of the sheet. Equity, or what you actually have, is also shown on the right side.

Assets = Liabilities + Equity is the mathematical formula for this.

Do you understand the distinction between an asset and a liability? To win the game of money accumulation, you must understand this distinction. Let's start with your current residence. Is that a plus or a minus?

According to Kiyosaki, if you responded asset (as most people do on their balance sheet), you are wrong. Why is this so? Because your home, even if it is free and clear, consumes money rather than putting money in your pocket. You must have a place to reside, which will always cost money. As a result, it is a liability in the strictest sense. According to Kiyosaki, an asset is something that puts money in your pocket. A liability is anything that deducts money from your bank account.

In Kiyosaki's vision, the biggest error that poor and middle-class individuals make is spending their life buying liabilities rather than assets. He teaches that if you want to be wealthy, all you have to do is spend your life buying assets.

Assets remind me of crops on a farm. Fruit trees, for example, are one of my favorite assets since they continue to produce harvests year after year. I don't have to tell you that real estate income properties are among the best fruit tree assets I've come across. Stocks, bonds, bank certificates of deposit, insurance annuities, and even your own business are all valid choices.

Basic investing strategies

An investment strategy is a plan for saving money to make it grow. All investments balance liquidity (the ease with which it can be changed into cash for other purposes), risk (the possibility that the investment will lose value), and prospective profits (how fast your investment can grow).

The balance of these three factors is up to your personal preference, but this balance will define the kind of investments you choose.

Security types

The security type is the type of investment you have. These can cover a wide spectrum, but every entire portfolio should include a couple of them.

- Cash and bank deposits

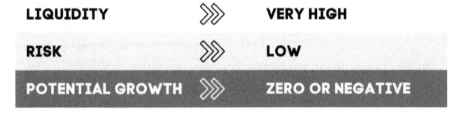

LIQUIDITY	VERY HIGH
RISK	LOW
POTENTIAL GROWTH	ZERO OR NEGATIVE

Cash, believe it or not, can be considered an investment in and of itself. Cash and bank deposits that may be withdrawn immediately are the most liquid assets because liquidity refers to how quickly you can turn any investment into cash.

The ability to utilize cash for whatever you choose is valuable, which is why "emergency funds" exist as cash and bank deposits rather than gold bars. On the other hand, cash does not expand and loses value over time due to inflation.

- Certificates of deposit

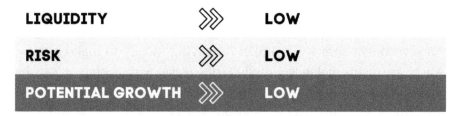

A Certificate of Deposit is similar to a savings account in that the interest rate is fixed, but you cannot withdraw the money for a set length of time. These are extremely safe investments, although they have very low growth potential.

- Stocks

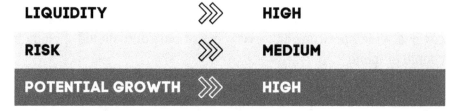

When most people think of investments, they think of stocks. Mutual funds and exchange-traded funds (ETFs) that hold equities all do the same thing in terms of investment strategy: they buy a piece of one or more companies in exchange for a percentage of their profits.

- Bonds

Bonds are classified into three types: corporate bonds, treasury bonds, and other government bonds. A bond, unlike stocks, is a loan made to a firm or government that must be repaid with interest. Corporate bonds and treasury bonds are typically relatively safe investments (thus the smaller yield), but there are also "Junk Bonds," or bonds with a higher risk of not being paid back in full. Organizations that sell Junk Bonds offer higher interest rates to customers who buy them in exchange for the higher risk.

- Real estate

LIQUIDITY	≫	LOW
RISK	≫	MEDIUM
POTENTIAL GROWTH	≫	MEDIUM

Land and buildings are examples of real estate. Until recently, most "retirement savings" took the shape of the home you lived in. People would buy a house and expect that the value would rise enough over the next 30-40 years to allow them to sell it and use the earnings to fund their retirement. Others buy damaged or inexpensive residences, repair them, and then resell them for a profit (a practice known as 'home flipping').

- Precious metals

LIQUIDITY	≫	HIGH
RISK	≫	MEDIUM
POTENTIAL GROWTH	≫	MEDIUM

This includes the purchase of gold and silver. Many people attempt to purchase gold and other precious metals as an investment (and to guard against inflation), but this has backfired in recent years as a "Gold Bubble" exploded, making metal prices more volatile than before. However, holding precious metals as a hedge against market instability in other forms of securities is still quite popular.

- Derivatives

LIQUIDITY	≫	MEDIUM
RISK	≫	HIGH
POTENTIAL GROWTH	≫	HIGH

Stock options and futures are examples of derivatives that ordinary investors can purchase. Being a "Derivative" indicates that its value is "derived" from something else — for example, a stock option has value since the stock that it allows you to buy has value (but the contract itself is useless unless you use it). Futures contracts are useful for commodities such as oil that will be supplied at a later date.

Derivatives are particularly beneficial for hedging (for example, buying a stock option on a stock you believe will rise in value but do not want to acquire right now).

Tips & Tricks

Many years ago, it was conventional investment advice to hold a significant portion of your "nest egg" in your home, which would mature with market rates if you were developing an investing strategy for retirement.

Financial experts would offer a "rule of thumb" to balance your assets between stocks and bonds based on your age for the remaining assets. Basically, take 100 and deduct your age to get the portion of your wealth in stocks (with the rest in bonds). This means that an 18-year-old would have 82 percent of their savings in bonds and 18 percent in cash.

This advice is a little out of date, but it contains a few critical nuggets of knowledge that all investors should be aware of.

• Diversifications
Divide your valuables among a few different levels of security. In the typical scenario, the saver would have around half of their assets in Real Estate, with the remaining half divided between Stocks and Bonds. This means that if property values decline, they will be protected because they have a large amount of money saved in stocks and bonds. If the stock market begins to tumble, they will be ok since they have their home and bonds. Current interest rates establish bonds' value; thus, they are shielded from this as well as

their other security types. On the other hand, they benefit if housing prices, stock prices, and interest rates rise.

- Evolving portfolio

The classic adage of "more bonds as you get older" is based on the assumption that your portfolio should become more conservative as you approach retirement. If you have a lot of stock that loses value when you're 25, you still have 40 years of income to compensate. If you have many equities that lose value when you're 62, it's far more difficult to replace that income.

Common investing strategies

There are a few major ones to bear in mind if you're ready to start investing. Most long-term investing methods rely on one or more of these.

- Purchase and hold

"If you aren't willing to hold a stock for ten years, don't even consider holding it for 10 minutes." - Warren Buffet

This strategy is founded on the premise that you undertake an extensive study of what you're buying, selecting your assets based on strong long-term rationale, then buying it and holding on to it regardless of market price fluctuations. For a "Buy and Hold" investor, the only time to sell is when:

1. When the underlying reasons for purchasing the stock change (for example, the company's management shifting to a team with a different business strategy that you dislike), or

2. When you intend to leave the industry totally

Negative aspects

"The market can stay irrational longer than you can stay solvent" — John M. Keynes

Even if all of your research is excellent, and even if the investment you made recovers its full value in the long run, you still have a deadline for when you will need that money to quit your job. You also run the risk of just being wrong in your decision, and with a Buy and Hold approach, you can absorb a significant loss before you admit to yourself that you have made a mistake.

- Value investing

"Know what you own, and know why you own it." —Peter Lynch

"Value Investing" seeks stocks that are undervalued in comparison to the rest of the market. This entails looking for companies that appear to be growing rapidly but have not yet gained much market attention, as well as new entrants with good foundations and growth prospects. With value investing, you will purchase and sell stocks more frequently — as soon as your picks appear to be "priced in" or "overvalued," you will consider selling and moving on.

Negative aspects

"The four most expensive words in the English language are, 'This time it's different.'" – John Templeton

Value investing necessitates paying close attention to companies you pick and re-evaluating how much you believe they are worth frequently. If you are incorrect several times in a row, you may have difficulty "bouncing back."

- Active investing

"Understanding the value of a security and whether it's trading above or below that value is the difference between investing and speculating." - Coreen T. Sol

"Active Trading" is when you buy and sell stock on a regular basis ("Day Trading" is when you buy and sell on the same day), hoping to profit from market volatility. Active trading necessitates a more advanced understanding of chart patterns, fundamental and technical analysis, and risk tolerance. In exchange, by riding market trends, you can generate enormous gains with active trading.

<u>Negative aspects</u>

"The individual investor should act consistently as an investor, rather than as a speculator." — Ben Graham

Active trading can produce significant gains quickly, but it may also produce large losses. Because the damage can be difficult to undo, most experienced investors and financial counselors advise using only a tiny amount of your portfolio for active trading.

Spending (Needs vs. Luxuries)

Regardless of household income, a considerable portion of U.S. expenditures are spent on what economists classify as luxuries. But how do we define necessities and luxuries?

If you were asked to construct a list of things you couldn't live without, your automobile, clothes dryer, and microwave would most certainly make the cut. However, if your parents were asked to make the same list when they were your age, they might have classed the same items as luxuries. As time passes, people believe they require more goods. It's not always simple to discriminate between what you need and what you want, but doing so might help you budget your money for the things you need and want most in life.

<u>Absolute Needs and Near Necessities</u>

There are two categories of demands: absolute needs and near necessities. You will perish if you do not meet your basic needs of food, clothing, and shelter. When we talk about needs, we do not mean that it is impossible to live without them. But without them in your life, it would be difficult, if not impossible, for you to study, work and contribute productively to your community. Near essentials include hygiene goods, cleaning supplies, and transportation.

Everyone has the same fundamental necessities, but what is a near requirement for you isn't always a near requirement for everyone else. For example, if you're studying in college, your textbooks are an immediate need, but if your friend has finished school and is working, books for him are extra.

Needs Across Time

The longer an item exists, the more people believe it to be a necessity. In 1996, most Americans considered computers, dishwashers, and air conditioners to be luxury items: things that made living easier but aren't required to get by. In 2010, however, the majority of Americans regarded all of those products to be essential. While you may need a home computer to conduct your homework or a cell phone in case of an emergency, thinking about what your parents or older siblings could manage without in the past can help you recognize expenses to decrease. For example, you may require a cell phone, but it does not imply that you require the latest model available with the best camera in the market, which is a luxury.

Needs Vary

Your concept of needs and luxuries will differ from your mother's, neighbor's, or brother's concept, but you may all utilize the same variables to calculate your particular requirements and wants. What's a need for you is determined by factors such as your location and work – or the job you want after you graduate. For example, while air conditioning is widespread in the United States, it is really a need only in warmer climates. Most individuals would like to have home Internet, but it is not required unless you work online or take online classes.

Budgeting

Whether you still live at home with your parents or have gone out on your own, creating a budget will help you be more disciplined with your money. Knowing the distinction between essentials and luxury is an important element of budgeting. Begin by outlining your absolute needs: the money you spend or contribute to your parents for housing, food, and clothing. Then, make a list of your immediate needs, including any school or extracurricular activity payments. Pay these bills first whenever you are paid or given money. Now write down a list of everything else you spend money on. These are your wishes. You can eliminate some of these expenses to begin saving money or avoid coming short when your estimated expenditure exceeds your income.

Planning a budget

Budgeting has a negative connotation among many American households, who see it as a means to take all of the enjoyment out of spending money. There will be no more shopping or eating out with friends.

That is not the purpose of budgeting. A budget simply indicates how much money is coming in and how that money is spent. It is one of the most helpful instruments in establishing a prosperous financial future since it allows you to get the most of your money.

Every consumer, regardless of economic status or generation, can benefit from developing and keeping a budget. A budget provides people with a sense of control over their finances. Consider a budget to be a financial foundation, which is unique for each person.

How to create a budget

Budgeting approaches differ from one another. There will be variances between what works for a first-year college student and what works for a retiree, for example. However, there are five fundamental elements to developing a budget. They are all important since they build on one another, assisting you in properly organizing your finances.

Establish goals

We can divide financial goals into two main categories: short-term goals and long-term goals. Immediate goals are concerned with how you will spend your money now, whereas long-term goals are concerned with saving and spending your money over time. Both are essential and work well together: Saving money today influences how much you spend now and how much you will have later in life.

It would be best if you decided which goals are for necessity and which are for luxury. You can then prioritize your financial objectives accordingly.

Covering current expenses is one of the most important financial goals. Some of these are required, such as your mortgage or rent, auto loans, utility bills, child care, food, cell phone, and household supplies. Non-essential apparel, subscriptions, dining out, and holidays are examples of secondary aims known as discretionary products. Long-term financial objectives may include retirement savings, investments, and charitable contributions. If you have debt, repaying it can be both obligatory and optional. Making required payments is critical to financial stability, but paying off debt early, while not needed, can save money in the long run.

Determine your earnings and expenses

After you've determined your financial objectives, you'll need a strategy for achieving them. To do so, you must first assess your income and spending. Because most bills are paid every month, most people budget monthly.

Begin by establishing a list of your monthly income sources, which should include your salary (after taxes), any regular bonuses, and child support or alimony payments. You can use an estimate if you don't know the actual number. Once you've gathered your data, add it all together. The sum represents your monthly revenue.

Your expenses are divided into fixed committed expenses, variable committed expenses, and discretionary spending.

Fixed committed expenses, such as your mortgage or rent, have a fixed monthly amount.

Variable committed expenses: These vary from month to month depending on necessity and include groceries and gasoline.

Discretionary expenses: As previously stated, these are optional costs that include amusement and entertainment. A gym membership is also included in this category. Discretionary costs can make life more enjoyable, but they should be the first to go if you can't afford the necessities.

If you don't pay off your credit card payments on time each month, you'll start paying a lot of interest. This may wreak havoc on any budget. If your carried-over credit card payments exceed 10% of your monthly income, you should consult with a nonprofit credit counselor. A free credit counseling consultation over the phone or online will walk you through your budget and identify expenses that can be decreased or eliminated. You may be able to lower your monthly debt payments if you qualify for a debt management program.

Examine your spending and balance your bank account

The purpose of budgeting is to keep your spending from exceeding your income. If they do, and you are spending more money than you earn, you must make changes. This does not necessarily imply that you should begin penny-pinching; rather, it is time to evaluate the discretionary expenditure category and determine where you are willing and able to reduce the expenses.

If you make payments by check, a checkbook register can help you keep track of your incoming and departing funds, as well as what you spend your money on. Although paying by check is becoming less common, individuals who use it should maintain their checkbooks balanced. This will save you money on overdraft fees and bounced checks, plus it will shed some light on your spending habits.

Here are the fundamentals:

• Keep track of all deposits and purchases. Fill out your check register, which the bank will supply you with.

• If you do not already receive a monthly bank statement in the mail, print or download one. If you're doing everything online, there's software that can make this — and budgeting — a breeze.

• Do your own calculations for deposits and withdrawals to ensure that your bank hasn't overlooked anything or cheated you out of money. Reconcile line by line, ensuring that your check record matches the statement.

• Work backward from the ending number on each monthly statement, checking to see what is clarified and what is not. Deposits that have not yet been clarified must be deducted from your balance. If your checks are not clarified either, they'll be added back to your account until they are.

• Account for any fees you are charged line by line. Seeing them up close may motivate you to contact and request that some be removed, which banks will usually do if you persevere. Include any interest pennies you may have received.

• Again, by simply using a computer or even a smartphone, you can automate this procedure with financial software or applications, which saves you lots of time and hassle. The idea is to go over your financial flow, look for mistakes, and learn from what you find.

Go over your original budget again

After you've had a month or two to track your income and expenditure, you'll be more aware of areas that need to be tweaked. Perhaps your initial monthly income calculations were incorrect, or you failed to account for expenses such as car repairs or veterinary expenditures. Make modifications, but always keep inflows and outflows in balance.

Once you've ironed out all the wrinkles in your budget, you must commit to sticking to it. However, because no budget lasts forever, regular reviews are essential for success.

If you got a pay raise, you could increase both your discretionary spending and your savings goals. A layoff or fewer work hours, on the other hand, may need a reduction in expenditure until your income is restored.

Savings should be an element of the strategy. Financial advisors recommend that you save six months' worth of income to cover a job loss or other disaster. You might find it helpful to start a second savings account and progressively fund it until you accomplish your goal. Maintaining a separate account makes it more difficult to dip into the emergency fund to cover non-essentials.

Commitment

Making a budget is an excellent first step toward a more financially secure future for you and your family. You'll get there if you stick to your budget. Maintain realism, examine it frequently, and don't be scared to adapt. Budgeting is all about finding a happy medium.

Benefits of budgeting

Everyone may benefit from taking a more assertive and proactive attitude to financial management. Sticking to your budget will help you get into a much better financial situation.

Budgeting can help you live a better life since it:

- Reveals waste

Making a budget sheds light on areas that many individuals overlook daily.

- Targets priorities

A budget enables people to look at the overall picture of their spending habits and set new priorities to optimize the potential of their money.

- Develops new habits

When consumers get a clearer image of how they've been spending their money, it allows them to categorize their spending and become more conscious of wasteful spending.

- Relieves stress

Money is always welcome but often proves to be a major source of stress. Instead, when you can have full control over the money coming in and the money going out, the tension can be transformed into a sense of power.

- Educates

A budget teaches people to see money as a tool, adjusting their perspective to focus on long-term goals and future requirements.

Planning a budget is the first step, but sticking to it is where you'll start to see true improvement in yourself and more money stretch. Sticking to a budget can be challenging for people who aren't used to spending limits or financial self-discipline, so it's critical to have a good attitude about the process. Keeping motivated might help reduce some of the financial stress. Consider putting money down each month to look forward to a quiet vacation at the end of the year.

Finally, define attainable objectives. Begin cautiously and gradually work your way up to a plan that works for you and your lifestyle.

Financial education

When we think about improving our financial condition, we usually focus on quick ways to get rich. It's all about making as much money as possible in the quickest length of time.

These types of ideas and methods, however, do not work for the majority of people. Typically, you must already have a reasonable amount of money saved and be willing to invest it and risk losing it.

A good financial future, like many other things, needs time, patience, and some education. I understand that this may not be what you want to hear, but let me explain why financial literacy is the most critical step on your path to financial wealth.

For a long time, many consumers have had little understanding of finances, how credit works, and the potential impact on financial well-being that poor financial decisions can cause. Indeed, a lack of financial knowledge has been identified as one of the primary reasons why many Americans struggle with saving and investing.

What Exactly Is Financial Literacy?

Financial literacy is the integration of financial, credit, and debt management knowledge required to make financially responsible decisions—choices that are essential in our daily lives. Knowing how a checking account works, what using a credit card truly means, and how to prevent debt are all examples of this knowledge. To summarize, financial literacy has a tangible influence on families as they attempt to balance their budgets, purchase a home, support their children's education, and assure a retirement income.

Although financial literacy varies with education and income, evidence suggests that highly educated customers with high incomes can be just as clueless about financial concerns as less-educated, lower-income people (although, in general, the latter tend to be less financially literate). Furthermore, consumers regard financial decision-making and education as complicated and anxiety-inducing.

Why financial literacy matters

Many people feel that financial planning is only for the wealthy, or at least the accountants who work for the wealthy. However, regardless of socioeconomic level, financial literacy and education are critical skills that everyone should begin cultivating at an early age. The more familiar you are with the financial world, the more steady you will be in life.

There is an increasing demand for financial education

Individuals must be able to grasp their financial status and make informed decisions now more than ever. As people struggle to stay up with the financial world, various causes make financial literacy a more critical ability.

Because people live longer lives, retirees will need more savings than earlier generations to maintain the same degree of comfort and financial stability.

The financial landscape is growing increasingly complex. Banks, credit unions, insurance firms, credit card companies, mortgage companies, and other financial service companies all compete for consumers' attention, adding to the confusion caused by the number of complex investment and savings products.

Government assistance is no longer adequate. Whereas past generations relied on Social Security monies during their retirement, the Social Security Trust Fund is expected to be totally exhausted by 2033. Most folks will not have enough savings to last their entire lifetimes if they do not plan ahead of time.

Income and financial literacy

Brown University professors analyzed information from various financial literacy studies, including a literacy survey that asked five fundamental financial questions to respondents of varying ages and experience levels. The data analysis generated some surprising but not unexpected outcomes. For example, only 5% of people between the ages of 18 and 24 correctly answered all financial literacy questions. However, comprehension appeared to improve with age, as 19% of those aged 65 and up aced the test.

The most important factor, however, seems to be household income. Twelve percent of persons earning $35,000 to $49,000 answered each question correctly, while 37 percent of those earning $150,000 or more achieved a perfect score. While more money does not guarantee greater financial literacy, it is reasonable to presume that those who are more economically successful have more financial education and practice.

Investing for retirement

According to a survey, 21 percent of respondents thought winning the lottery was the most practical technique for saving for retirement. Not only is such an outcome statistically implausible, but it also demonstrates how little the general public understands the need for planning and preparing for the future. Workplace 401(k) plans and diversified stock portfolios are among the most secure and effective saving strategies available. Because most Americans have a low degree of financial literacy, better financial education could stimulate more personal savings, enhancing financial and economic security throughout life and into retirement.

What changed in 2021

Among the many unintended consequences of the Covid-19 pandemic was the financial impact it had on primarily low- and middle-income people and populations already considered financially vulnerable, such as migrants living in the United States.

Many of these people found themselves without jobs and were dependent on government help, such as stimulus checks, which took a long time to arrive, assuming they were even eligible for them at all. For example, families with mixed immigration status were barred from obtaining incentive grants, despite being among the populations most in need.

In January 2020, before the full consequences of the pandemic were seen in the United States, 41 percent of Americans claimed that they would be unable to meet a $1,000 emergency with their savings. Six months later, as the virus ravaged the United States, over 25% of Americans had no emergency reserves at all, and 16% had taken on more debt since the pandemic began. Furthermore, roughly one-third reported a decreased income than six months previous.

Although being more financially savvy may not have completely reduced the financial burden caused by the coronavirus, it may have assisted many people in being better prepared. That is why we feel you should make 2021 your year to become financially smart!

Benefits of financial education

Being financially educated is a skill that provides many benefits that can improve an individual's standard of living by increasing financial security.

Here are some of the advantages of financial literacy:

- Ability to make sound financial decisions
- Effective management of money and debt
- More capable of achieving financial objectives
- Expense reduction through improved control
- Reduction of financial stress and worry
- Enhance ethical decision-making when purchasing insurance, taking out loans, investing, or using a credit card.
- Ability to create a structured budget

How to improve your financial literacy

What are the most effective strategies for increasing your financial literacy? Whether you live for complex investing techniques and tax-advantaged strategies or can't tell the difference between ETFs and HSAs, it's vital to understand the fundamentals and learn about the resources that can help you make the best financial decisions.

Fortunately, there is no shortage of tools available to assist you in taking your financial knowledge to the next level. Below are some of the best ways you can start building your financial education

<u>Read a good book</u>

An excellent book is an obvious place to start for anyone attempting to develop financial literacy. The main advantages of print are that you may move at your own pace and focus on the most interesting things. Of course, any excellent library will have a large collection to choose from, but here are a few highly respected titles to get you started.

- "Personal Finance for Dummies" by Eric Tyson
- "The Only Investment Guide You'll Ever Need" by Andrew Tobias
- "Why Didn't They Teach Me This in School?" by Cary Siegel
- "The Richest Man in Babylon" by George S. Clason
- "Blueprint to a Billion: 7 Essentials to Achieve Exponential Growth" by David G. Thomson

<u>Get a financial magazine subscription</u>

With so much fantastic content available on the internet, paying for a print magazine may appear to be an archaic method. However, receiving a publication in your mailbox every week or month prevents you from sliding off the financial wagon for too long. Furthermore, publications have a way of introducing you to topics and ideas that you might not have found on your own. The resources listed below are some of the best for improving your financial knowledge.

- The Economist
- Kiplinger's
- Forbes
- Investor's Business Daily
- Barron's
- Money

Listen to a podcast

Whether you're driving, going for a jog, or doing housework, podcasts are a convenient method to learn about money management without putting in any effort. Spotify has revealed that podcast listening has more than doubled since the pandemic disrupted everyone's schedules and listening habits. This is a clear indication that everyone is looking for information, assistance, or just plain entertainment.

Money-related podcasts are incredibly hot right now. Because the podcasting landscape is so congested, I'm recommending my favorite titles.

- So Money
- Side Hustle Pro.
- Afford Anything
- BiggerPockets Money
- Planet Money
- Future Rich

Discover community events

In-person and virtual events are another way to improve your financial literacy and begin making better financial decisions. Seminars given by local financial specialists, for example, are sometimes held at public libraries. Many of these events include question-and-answer sessions where you can obtain particular guidance on a financial situation you're facing.

Several community-based financial literacy programs across the country provide a variety of tools geared toward low- and middle-income individuals, such as budgeting and investment seminars. In addition, some organizations offer free counseling sessions for qualified participants, during which you can speak one-on-one with a financial coach.

Long-Term vs. Short-Term

Everyone has financial goals, some of which are short-term, like purchasing a car, and others that are long-term, such as saving for a child's education or retirement. But how can we meet both without compromising one? Can we attain our long-term objectives while simultaneously meeting our immediate needs?

How to achieve both short- and long-term financial goals

In an ideal world, we'd all put our investable cash into a long-term investment account and continue to increase those assets by contributing as much as we can over the next several decades. If we all stick to this plan, our major financial decisions will revolve around optimizing our returns in changing market circumstances, keeping risks within our comfort zone, and managing related taxes. Then, voilà, we'll all have a nice nest egg to fuel our futures.

If only it were that easy.

Life happens over those "many decades" that you are saving for your future, and investing decisions become a little more challenging. For example, you may require funds for a down payment on a house, a new car, or a sudden bill such as dental surgery. So, how do we strike a compromise between our short-term savings goals and our longer-term ones, which investment will almost certainly help us achieve our goal?

Setting goals for short- vs. long-term savings

These opposing short- and long-term objectives necessitate additional consideration for your investible assets' appropriate positioning. Therefore, when determining how to balance your short- and long-term savings goals, the first thing to ask yourself is: what precise short-term goals are you attempting to attain, and when will you want the funds?

There is no one-size-fits-all solution since, in addition to the practically limitless items people save for in the short term, there are several other variables to consider beyond when you need the money. For example, you should consider your timeline's flexibility, risk tolerance, and even the urgency or relevance of your aim.

As an example, consider a down payment on a house. How much do you require? Let's say you have $120,000. When will you require it? We'll go for four years. Is homeownership a pressing or vital goal for you at this time in your life? Maybe, maybe not, or maybe the amount needs to be adjusted. However, the answers to these questions will decide how much you need to save and when and how much risk you are willing to take with the money to reach your deadline. These are decisions that you can make with the guidance of a financial counselor, depending on your unique circumstances.

After you've clearly selected a realistic objective and defined the amount, duration, and urgency of the goal, the next step is to determine where to invest your money to optimize its worth while you work toward achieving your objective. There are no strict rules here, though, so the advice of a financial expert can be invaluable.

Guidelines based on when you will need your money

You're probably wondering, "What exactly is a short-term goal?" How brief is the word "short-term"?

A short-term objective is often defined as anything you will need money in less than 18 months. We recommend allocating savings towards a short-term aim as follows:

If you need the money in less than 18 months, consider opening a safe, liquid savings account to keep your money FDIC guaranteed and immediately available to fulfill your goal.

A "mid-term" aim is something for which you will need funds in the next 18 to 36 months. Here's how we advocate saving towards mid-term goals:

If you want finances in the next 18 to 36 months

Your choice may be influenced by how much of your net worth the goal sum reflects.

If the sum is less than 10% of your net worth, your best bet is to stick with your existing plan or to adopt a somewhat less aggressive but still long-term plan for some ambitions.

If the amount represents more than 10% of your net worth and your timeframe is rigid, consider high-yield savings account to keep the assets safe and accessible.

You won't need the money for more than 36 months

Anything that will not necessitate cash for longer than 36 months is generally regarded as a long-term saving aim. Again, your choices may be influenced by the impact of the targeted amount on your net worth.

If the sum is less than 10% of your net worth, your best bet is to keep your money invested in accordance with your present investment strategy.

If the amount exceeds 10% of your net worth, you should consider shifting the money to a more cautious long-term investing strategy, especially if your current investment style is aggressive. However, if you have some time on your side, you may choose to remain with your existing investment approach.

<u>Emergency fund</u>

As an emergency reserve, I normally recommend keeping three to six months' worth of living expenses in cash. It is critical to have funds ready in the event of a job loss, severe medical bill, or other emergency crisis. But don't let your money sit in regular savings or checking account; instead, put it to work in a high-interest account to generate interest on the money you've set aside for emergencies.

My advice

While these recommendations are helpful, ultimately, it is up to you. I wish I could give you firm counsel, but when it comes to investing and personal money, "one-size-fits-all" counsel rarely works. So, remember to consider the urgency of your goal, your schedule, and how all of this fits with your investing approach. For example, how rigid is your goal? Is it a "must" to be in a property within five years in the case we mentioned earlier – the down payment – or could you wait longer? What is your level of risk tolerance? Will you be concerned every time the market takes a turn if you keep your goal money invested for the long term?

Now assess those factors against how your choices will affect your capacity to complete your task. Putting assets in a savings account that will not be needed for more than 36 months, for example, may feel safe, but it is likely counterproductive due to opportunity costs. While you wait to spend your money, it will not grow significantly. Will foregoing possible returns on your money cause you to miss your goal?

For most investors and many goals with a mid-to-long-term time horizon, it is definitely worth the risk of maintaining a long-term investment strategy to profit from the higher return potential. Your advisor can assist you in determining your specific risk tolerance and the ideal location to park cash for your various financial goals so that you may work towards them comfortably – whether they are short or long term.

Developing a successful money mindset

The most significant aspects of your financial life are not your bank account, investment strategy, or credit score. Your net worth isn't even the most important factor. Your mindset is the most crucial aspect of your financial life.

Those other performance criteria are meaningless unless you have the correct way of thinking and feeling about your financial well-being. A positive mentality leads to positive habits and a positive relationship with money. Without this fundamental approach to financial management, all the great planning and execution in the world will not improve your entire life. Having the proper money mindset entails:

Forming an abundance mindset

Much of the world lives in a scarcity mindset. Scarcity is at the root of the financial crisis, global warfare, and fear-based media. They believe that your good fortune is in jeopardy since the opportunity is limited. A mindset of abundance accepts these dangers but recognizes that there will be additional chances if you plan and execute wisely. Adopting an abundance mindset is what brings the good things in life, so be sure that more good awaits those who plan and act correctly to achieve their objectives.

A smart strategy to develop your abundant mindset is to reframe any intruding, negative thoughts that occur when you are anxious as wonderful opportunities rather than threats.

Anticipating your nature

Knowing yourself and being honest about who you are is an essential part of having a good financial mentality. We are all impulsive, emotional, and messy people. Creating extremely strict budgets that don't allow for your odd urge can derail all of your attempts to better your financial situation. Deprivation can cause you to lash out and hate your efforts in impulsive ways, resulting in overcharges and other unpleasant effects.

Know what your impulsive vices are and make plans to eliminate them in healthy ways while still rewarding yourself on occasion. Whether it's an impulsive purchase of a discounted ebook or a once-a-month trip to the movies, you must allow yourself to enjoy life while working toward financial wellness.

Coping with adversities

Success is never a straight line, and neither is your financial trend line. Changing your habits, investing, and attempting to improve your financial situation all have dangers. Can you live with negative returns on higher-risk investments? Can you manage your money like a business and accept that your money will be working for you in multiple places? Accepting the ongoing existence of change and uncertainty while maintaining confidence in your strategy's ability to work for you is critical for your attitude.

Automated investment and savings solutions can help you with this by keeping it out of sight and out of mind. Market downturns and setbacks are unavoidable, but the key is to remain confident in your excellent approach in the face of market turbulence, which might affect your investments.

Keeping focused

Staying in the process and focusing on the positive outcomes you're aiming for is simple early on in your financial journey. Can you keep that focus throughout the year? What, five years? Figuring out what steps you need to take to stay motivated and work toward financial success is critical for your path. It's a moving target that necessitates brutal honesty with oneself, but staying motivated is critical. Some people utilize vision boards or other simple reminders of their goals.

Some people keep note of their behavior patterns on a calendar or via a smartphone app. What works best for you will not work for everyone else; you simply need to figure out how to keep yourself motivated naturally and efficiently.

<u>Expressing gratitude</u>

Being grateful for what you have now and for the future you are constructing will be highly beneficial. Too many people live their lives negatively and jaded, resenting their existing situation but doing little to change it. It extends beyond simply appreciating what you have. Genuine appreciation entails appreciating the good fortunes of others and contributing to a better world via self-improvement. You are your most important asset, and you should be grateful for the commitment you are making to yourself and your life as you embark on this journey to a better financial life.

The bottom line

Financial wealth will not be an issue for you if these principles are consistently worked on and built upon. These basics have endured the test of time and will continue to function for as long as you do.

Consider a world in which you will never have to worry about money again. Think about how that would make you feel, how it would alter your interactions with the world and the people around you, how it might affect your family situation, and so on. Isn't it a fantastic feeling? It is entirely possible to live this kind of life one day if you commit to achieving financial wealth as well as the three other sorts of riches.

Chapter Three

SOCIAL WEALTH

S ince we don't conceive status as a form of wealth, social wealth or status is one of the most undervalued sorts of riches. We recognize that status has worth, but we never connect the dots that it is a form of money.

The truth is that the society we live in tends to shape our ideas and attitudes towards certain groups of people. However, this must be viewed in a new light. For example, we frequently equate business people with corruption and falsehoods, but this is a worldview imposed on our brain by those around us. You can become a successful person, and as long as you don't use it to gain power and dominance over others, you will be respected.

People tend to follow, listen to, and respect you if you are perceived as a dominant member of a group. We actually do want people to look up to us, as much as we pretend we don't want them to; however, that's a natural tendency in human beings, for heroes and social domination have existed since ever. Yet, it's a two-way street, and just because you admire someone doesn't make you better or worse; you just prefer to follow as an example of his/her general behavior. So, what will assist you in achieving this level of wealth?

<u>Being confident and secure in your words</u>

No one appreciates a braggart, someone who seeks the spotlight and battles for either the Jedis or the Dark Force. When you enter a discussion, you must be prepared and know exactly what you're talking about. Though you should listen to other people's opinions and possibly adjust your own, don't do so to seem a good person; instead, strive to contribute to the overall view.

Be a good listener and a good talker

Being a good listener makes you a great friend. So, if you truly care about someone, express it by standing up for them. On the other side, if you are in a leadership position, listen to your employees while also learning how to communicate with them and guide them towards your perspective.

Attention: This does not imply that you should impose an "undercover dictatorship," but you may be in a better position to see the common good rather than someone who is not a leader, and it is your responsibility to gather opinions and viewpoints to accomplish the goals. Persuasion will get you there.

Be true to yourself

In other words, be a man of your word. One of the most admirable characteristics is trustworthiness. Someone who follows their promises till the end and does not give up at the first setback is always admired and respected. You also need to respect others along the journey and understand when to give up but don't give up without a fight if you're guiding someone.

Spam isn't just sent to you

Everyone has a life and deals with it in different ways, and being someone with whom others feel at ease is so precious. Everyone admires an understanding person.

All of these factors will help you develop a reputation around you, a successful reputation on which you should remain humble throughout the process. Having it all does not make you perfect or less human; it simply sharpens your perspective on life.

Creating and sustaining social wealth requires a full understanding of some key elements. Let's look at them together.

Persuasion skill

Persuasion skills are a valuable asset in all aspects of our lives. The capacity to persuade others, provide persuasive arguments, and persuade people to act is a valued trait that can be useful in a variety of settings. If you want to learn how to enhance your persuasive talents, you must first understand what the phrase entails.

This chapter will address the topic in the workplace context, but the principles expressed are valid in any other social setting.

Persuasion is the process of persuading someone else to do something or agree to an idea. Persuasion is used in the workplace to sell items, recruit team members, and boost productivity. Employees with great persuasion abilities can persuade others to work hard and succeed. A convincing employee can also help to speed up and simplify collective decision-making. Persuasion is a valuable soft talent that, when utilized correctly, can have a big impact in any situation. It requires some specific soft skills

Soft skills required to master the art of persuasion

<u>Communication</u>

Good communication skills serve as the foundation for developing other persuasive abilities. The purpose of being persuasive is to persuade people to think or act in a certain manner, and speaking with them is the easiest way to do it. Effective communication abilities include being able to explain yourself clearly, employing non-verbal gestures, and utilizing vocabulary that the other person understands. If you can present your ideas and thoughts in an entertaining manner that appeals to your listener, they will be more likely to be persuaded.

Social and emotional intelligence

Another crucial persuasive talent is the ability to detect and comprehend your listener's emotions. Emotional intelligence is an acquired talent that helps you to recognize and respond to the emotions of others. When utilized for persuasion, it also assists you in tailoring your persuasive approaches to a certain situation or person.

Assume you're trying to persuade one of your coworkers to take on new job responsibility. You see that their arms are crossed and that they are avoiding eye contact as you speak to them. When they speak, their phrases are brief and to the point. You should be able to tell if they are upset or intimidated by using your emotional intelligence. You will be able to adapt your persuasion strategies based on this information in order to try to calm them down or alleviate their anxieties.

Listening actively

Active listening is another taught persuasive skill. Listening well entails paying attention and being respectful in your interactions with others. Before you can persuade someone, you must first learn about and comprehend their worries or arguments. Allowing the other person time to talk and share their opinions can make them feel respected and help create trust. It will also help you understand their motivations, which will allow you to create more effective persuasive arguments.

Reasoning and logic

Many compelling arguments are constructed using logic and reasoning skills. Before you can persuade someone to believe in a concept or commit to an action, they must understand why doing so is the best option. To demonstrate this, you must argue with them using facts that support your point of view. A logical mentality and strong reasoning abilities will assist you in developing convincing persuasive arguments.

<u>Interpersonal skills</u>

Interpersonal skills are built on your ability to communicate positively with others and sustain meaningful relationships. Persuasion may be difficult for you if you are not comfortable initiating discussions or engaging in professional relations. Being real, natural, and at least a bit charismatic are all aspects of being persuasive. People are more inclined to agree with someone they like, thus strengthening your interpersonal ties is one of the best methods to improve your persuasion skills.

<u>Negotiating</u>

Negotiation is frequently an essential component of successful persuasion. In many circumstances, the person you're trying to persuade will refuse to comply unless they believe they'll benefit from the arrangement. To encourage them to join, you may need to be able to mediate a compromise. To accomplish this, you will need to understand their needs, discover a strategy to address those needs, and negotiate an acceptable agreement with all parties.

Negotiation skills need experience, but they may be quite useful when trying to persuade a recalcitrant teammate or client.

How to use persuasion skills

It will take time, work, and practice to successfully execute your persuasion talents. Here are some pointers on how to properly persuade others.

Concentrate on trust

One of the most crucial aspects of persuasive dialogues is the development of trust. If you ask someone else to take a risk or step outside of their comfort zone, they must trust you and your judgment. You must keep a good reputation in your company and be willing to serve to create trust. Others are more inclined to return the favor if you demonstrate selflessness and willingness to help.

Keep an eye on your surroundings

Choosing the right time and place is an important part of staging a successful persuasive dialogue. You'll want to pick a venue where your listener will feel at ease. This might take place in your office, the staff area, a neighboring coffee shop, or even your own house. You should also choose a moment when they are not anxious or rushed, such as the beginning of the week or over a long lunch break.

Look for things you have in common

It is critical to identify common ground between yourself and your listeners as you begin a compelling conversation or presentation. Concentrate on your common challenges or similar aspirations. If you can find something on which you both agree right away, the audience will be more open to your other ideas.

Use of facts and emotions

When persuading someone, you must give irrefutable evidence that demonstrates how agreeing with you would benefit them. For example, you may persuade the buyer by displaying graphs with specific safety data if you're selling a car. To appeal to their emotions, you could tell the same customer how much fun it would be to drive their kids in the automobile on family road trips—and even if the kids aren't having fun, they're in a safe vehicle.

How to sharpen your persuasion skills

There are various actions you can take to improve your persuasion skills:

Focus on developing relationships

Improving your people skills is the first step toward more successful persuasion. Concentrate on establishing trust and rapport with employees, clients, and friends. Even if you never have to utilize your persuasion talents on these people, building stronger relationships with them will allow you to exercise your interpersonal and emotional intelligence talents. You can also look for opportunities to meet new people and expand your professional network.

Increase your self-assurance

If you want to convince somebody to change their mind or commit to a task, you must be completely confident in your reasoning. If you have difficulty making eye contact or expressing yourself clearly, your listener will have difficulty trusting your argument. Practice your persuasive presentations ahead of time, and remove nonverbal cues that make you appear uncomfortable.

Hone your communication abilities

Developing your professional and personal communication abilities necessitates being mindful of how you communicate with people. Seek out opportunities to start or participate in conversations. Make an effort to participate in group decisions and workplace meetings. Any chance you get to become a better communicator will also help you become a better persuasive speaker.

Reputation

We can define our reputation as the sum of our actions and what others say about us. This simple formula is the most effective leverage you have in business – and, for that matter, in life.

While some suggest you shouldn't worry about what others think, I'm skeptical of that advice. Others often decide your fate, whether it's a vendor offering you a great bargain, a recruiting manager considering granting you a position, or someone with purchasing power. It only takes a slight nudge from a trusted source to either get you in or push you out.

Today, we must consider reputation management even more than in the past. Not only we must be concerned with how we show ourselves in person, but also with how we appear online. I'm not here to teach you the fundamentals, such as how to avoid immature or inappropriate stuff on social network websites. Hopefully, you are aware of this. Instead, I'm here to remind you to make a good first impression in person and then leverage that effort to build a strong reputation currency online. Here are some guidelines to help you achieve this goal.

Keep your promises

It sounds so simple, but think about it: how often have you asked your banker to send you something, your assistant to pick something up, or your vendor to contact you back, only to be ignored? You must then remember to follow up and hope they maintain their promises. Consider an instance when someone promised to do something and then followed through. You probably associate them with dependability and dependability. You have faith in them. And you'd almost certainly give them a strong recommendation or referral, right? Aspirationally, you should be that person.

Help others achieve their goals

Being respected entails more than just being concerned with yourself and your personal success. Develop a mindset of service to others. Is your friend's child at college and interested in learning more about the business world? Offer to speak with them for a few minutes to offer advice and answer questions. Do you have any sales contacts who are seeking a good deal? Inquire whether you can assist them by making the appropriate introduction. Is one of your colleagues had to leave 30 minutes early due to a family obligation? Offer to stand in for them.

Make others look good

Have you ever unintentionally harmed someone with your behavior? It's not pleasant, is it? Developing strategies to make others look good is key to improving your reputation. Have you been referred to a company as a potential client or for a job? As a thank you, make them feel important! Arrive early, be prepared, and listen carefully to everything they have to say. This will help your reputation grow, making the referral feel proud to have introduced you.

Go beyond your mere duty

Have you received a request for a reference? Make three suggestions. Did you promise a client that you would save them 10%? Make a 20% discount. Did you say you would respond within 24 hours? Send an email with the response after a few hours. Send a handwritten thank-you note if you had a satisfactory business meeting. These small actions that cost you little will actually make you remembered as reliable and pleasant people.

Take care of the first impression

Your initial impression is an often disregarded and even underrated aspect of your reputation. Whether you like it or not, people form opinions about you even before you open your mouth and start talking. Clothing plays an important role in creating the first impression. So make sure you wear appropriate clothes for the occasion. Don't be too relaxed. If you're not sure what dress code to follow, always err on the side of being overdressed. Make certain that your clothing is clean, wrinkle-free, well-fitting, and current. Make sure your hair is well-groomed, and if you wear makeup, that it is not obtrusive. Don't pass up an opportunity to impress someone because you don't dress appropriately.

Make your body language matter

People can know a lot about you just by your body language. Make sure your body is facing your audience, your feet are pointed in their direction, and you have a tall stance. Nod your head in agreement, occasionally leaning against the other person, and grin here and there.

This topic is so important to your reputation that we'll cover it specifically in the next few pages.

Maintain consistency

Being inauthentic will not help you since you will be unable to maintain consistency. You must demonstrate the same outstanding attributes to everyone you meet, even on difficult days. Your reputation will suffer if you are terrific in one situation but harsh, unpleasant, and/or cold in another. People are significantly more likely to relate negative experiences than happy ones. And, as you may be aware, they may spread swiftly.

Act with honesty

Everything you do should be based on this principle. Small acts of greed, selfishness, and envy can work against you (in ways you may not even recognize) and make your lack of integrity obvious, especially in the business world. If you wouldn't buy the business you're selling, then you shouldn't even try to sell it. Another very common example? It's not honest to promise someone to respond by a certain date if you already know you won't be able to.

Participate in your community

Your neighborhood can be as little as your business or as vast as your metropolis. Your engagement will be entirely determined by your values and objectives. Being engaged entails getting to know people, volunteering your time and resources, and making yourself available.

<u>Make an effort to be liked</u>

Being likable is inextricably linked to being yourself. When you approach someone you don't know, offer a handshake and smile. All of these minor details can help you become more likable. Being fake is what makes you unlikable. Be careful not to misrepresent yourself in order to look nice.

People in your life who exhibit most or all of these characteristics are likely to be those you hold in the highest consideration. Their reputation precedes them (in a good way), and they don't need to sell their qualities or brag because their good reputation is doing it all for them. Undoubtedly, there is no greater value than a positive reputation because it will allow you to have opportunities that you might have never had without it.

Body Language

Simply said, body language is the unspoken element of communication through which we express our genuine feelings and emotions.

The relaxed facial expression bursts out into a real smile, with the mouth tilted and the eyes wrinkled. It can be as simple as a head tilt to indicate that you're listening, sitting or standing upright to express interest or directing attention with hand gestures. It can also mean avoiding a defensive, arms-crossed posture or tapping your foot restlessly.

When you can "read" signs like this, you can comprehend the full message of what someone is saying to you. You'll be more conscious of how other people react to what you say and do. You'll also be able to change your body language to appear more upbeat, engaged, and friendly.

If you don't think it's relevant, here's another way to put it: Examine your posture and how you're sitting or standing right now. What is your expression like? Do you have a scowl or a smile on your face? Are you sitting or slouching in your chair? What do you believe people would say about you if they took a snapshot of you right now based on your current body language? Will they say you appear pleasant and approachable, or will they say you're not to be trifled with?

Body language is mostly unconscious, which means that you can vocally agree or disagree with something while your body language says the exact opposite.

People will frequently try to appear confident, but their body language will reveal otherwise. Or they'll say something like, "I'm glad and pleased to be here," but their facial expressions and movements indicate otherwise. If you're out somewhere and meet a bunch of new people, you may tell them you're happy to meet them, even though your body language actually suggests the opposite. You might believe you performed admirably in that social circumstance. However, the folks you just met probably won't remember you since something about your body language didn't set well with them.

The simple truth is that body language is famous for revealing our true feelings. We may not say anything out loud, and we may even strongly reject something, but our body language will reveal to the world what we truly think or believe about something or someone.

The importance of body language

According to research, when people express their likes and dislikes, around 93 percent of communication is nonverbal, including your body language and tone. Body language accounts for 55 percent of communication in specific situations, tone for 38 percent, and words for a meager 7 percent.

This amount is only a rough estimate based on a few specific studies and circumstances analyzed, but it still serves as an important lesson. The way you hold yourself is often more significant than the things you say. People will almost always believe your body language and tone of voice over your words. Let me give you an example. For a good reason, my friend Jack was becoming irritated with his wife. She had betrayed his faith! "I'm weary of how you treat me, and I'm not going to put up with it any longer," he stated. "I'm weak, fully fired up, and going to put up with you treating me like this forever," his tone (high pitched, fast speaking, and furious) and body language (he was feverishly pacing, not making eye contact, and even shriveled) indicated. So did you notice how body language matters? Body language is probably the most fundamental aspect of any communication. So make sure your body language is in line with your statements and objectives.

Body language and subconscious

You may be wondering how only 7% of communication occurs through words, given we place so much emphasis on them. The rationale is straightforward: understanding body language occurs outside of conscious awareness. For example, if you receive a "weird vibe" from someone, it's most likely due to subconscious body language interpretation.

If you find someone attractive, the way they carry themselves likely plays a significant factor in why you like them. This is also why people who positively change their body language (for example, by improving their posture and standing up straight) frequently receive comments like "something is different about you...but I can't tell what !" and here's where they start to get more attention from others.

When people adjust/correct their body language, most of them notice an immediate difference in their interpersonal relations. If our bodies and intonation are responsible for 93 percent of our communication, then even minor improvements will provide tremendous effects.

But since, as we said earlier, body language is a process that takes place in our subconscious, most people are unaware of how they appear to others.

How to improve your body language for success

While on trial in Athens, Socrates famously said, "The unexamined life is not worth living." The majority of people have no idea of how they really appear to others. They may stoop, walk with their heads down, show insecurity and hesitancy in their bodies despite using powerful words.

Become aware of your body language right now. Are you at ease? Are you ready? Are you certain? Or are you self-conscious? Closed? Do you feel insecure? The good news is that you can adjust your body language and so "hack" how others see you.

For many people, this may be as simple as raising your head slightly (signaling confidence) instead of looking down when conversing with others. As you gradually "hack" your body's movements and posture, people will respect you more and will find you more appealing, even if they don't realize it.

Boost your self-esteem with more confident body language

Even if you aren't feeling confident, using confident body language can boost your self-esteem and make you feel better about yourself. Here are seven ways to increase your confidence through body language.

Make direct eye contact

This isn't merely an old wives' tale or an old-fashioned custom. Numerous psychological processes at work contribute to the strength of eye contact between two people.

Maintain eye contact in social encounters to appear confident. Good eye contact communicates to people that you are interested and at ease. About 60% of the time, look the other person in the eyes. If making direct eye contact is too daunting, begin by glancing at a point near the person's eyes.

Firmly shake hands

How does your handshake look? A shaky or limp handshake is an evident indicator of insecurity, so practice offering a solid handshake when meeting new people. With practice, it will soon become a completely natural habit.

Lean forward

Leaning forward in a conversation demonstrates interest and attention. While it may be tempting to keep your distance if you are socially apprehensive, this sends the sense that you are uninterested or aloof.

Stand up straight

Don't slouch! Those who lack self-confidence tend to take up as little space as possible, including sitting stooped over in a protective posture. Straighten your spine, move your shoulders away from your ears, and uncross your arms and legs.

First, you'll feel and appear more confident, providing you an advantage in a dialogue. Second, you'll instinctively adopt a more "open" and friendly demeanor. Finally, it will allow you to breathe more fully and healthily during the talk, providing your words more strength and more oxygen to your lungs.

Chin-up

Do you gaze down at the ground while you walk? Is your chin always bowed? Instead, walk with your head held high and your gaze forward. It may feel strange at first, but you will grow accustomed to this more confident posture.

Keep your hands out of your pockets

Even though you sometimes find it natural to keep your hands in your pockets, especially if you are concerned that they will shake, doing so makes you appear uneasy. Keep your hands out of your pockets to appear more self-confident.

Slow down your movement

You appear more worried if you move quickly. Everything from your walking stride to your hand gestures can make a difference; slow down and watch how you feel more confident.

Don't fidget

Fidgeting is a clear indication of worry and uneasiness. Keep fidgeting to a minimum to appear more confident. Nervous gestures divert attention away from what you're saying and make it difficult for people to concentrate on your message.

Take longer steps

When you walk, attempt to take longer steps as you slow down. Self-assured people take larger steps and walk with authority. You will feel less worried as a result of doing so.

Keep an eye on your hands

Avoid touching your face or neck; both are indicators that you are worried, apprehensive, or terrified. These are not the movements of confident people.

Still unsure if you can generate the courage to alter your body language? Remember that you do not need to be self-assured to change your behavior. Although it may feel uncomfortable at first, acting confidently will become more natural and may even increase your self-esteem.

If you really need proof, watch yourself on camera; once you identify your nervous patterns and posture, you can simply change them. Simultaneously, reducing your worry through other means will have a natural influence on reducing tense behaviors.

Body language tips when meeting new people

For many people, dating and meeting new people can be a stressful experience. However, others find it to be an exciting and instructive process. In any case, you will meet new people in your life, and it is in your best interest to make an excellent first impression.

Making a good first impression isn't always easy, especially if you're in a new place or don't know what to say.

There are, however, a few body language "hacks" you may use to ensure a pleasant reception, participate in a decent conversation, and eventually walk away with a warm, new acquaintance. Some coincide with those already analyzed in the previous paragraph (making eye contact, standing up straight); now, let's see the others.

Strike a powerful pose

This hack occurs before you even enter the room. According to research, "power poses" can fool your brain into feeling more confident, resulting in smoother conversation and a more poised demeanor. Standing tall and raising your fists in the air, or taking up space by putting your hands on your hips, is what this means. Do this for 30 to 60 seconds, and you'll find yourself walking into the room feeling naturally more confident.

Keep an "open" stance

Your body's position might reveal a lot about what you're thinking or feeling. People will assume you don't want to talk if your body posture is "closed," such as when your head is down, or your arms are folded. However, if your posture is "open," you will be perceived as welcome and kind with your shoulders back and your head up.

Make contact (when appropriate)

Touching someone establishes an instant connection with him or her, which is why shaking hands leaves a lasting impact when you first meet someone. Give a handshake and, where appropriate, make additional types of physical contact, such as a touch on the shoulder of your new acquaintance. Just remember to keep it appropriate: Unwanted touch, particularly in male-female relations, might have more negative than positive power.

Gesticulate

Making occasional gestures with your arms and hands can help make your remarks more interesting to others. Punching the air can help you highlight a particular point. If you wish to solicit someone's opinion, an upward-turned hand can make the request more appealing.

The only risk here is not the kinds of movements you can use but the frequency with which you utilize them. Too much gesturing will make you appear insane. So, keep your gestures to a minimum.

Remain still

It is unnecessary to stay totally still during the interaction; doing so can make you appear robotic. However, it would be best if you avoided any movement that disrupts the dialogue. Tapping your foot, pacing around, or wringing your hands, for example, can make you appear uncomfortable and unconfident. Instead, attempt to maintain as much control over yourself (and your appendages) as possible. This behavior will make you look more confident.

These body-language techniques won't make up for a boring discussion or a harsh disposition, but they will get you off to a great start with almost everyone. If you're still unsure about these tricks, try them out in front of the mirror or with family members and friends until you get the hang of them.

Don't worry if these hacks look forced at first; they will become natural with more practice over time. You may meet anyone, anywhere at that moment, and your body language will respond automatically.

Winning personality

Our personality and character have a significant influence on how others see and regard us.

Every personality type has strengths and faults - there is no perfect type, just as there are no perfect people on this earth. That being said, it is almost unavoidable that you will declare at some point in your life, "I wish I had a different personality." You might desire to become more outgoing, in tune with your senses, more organized, more resistant to criticism, and so on. Not surprisingly, one of the most often asked personal development questions is, "Can I change my personality type?"

Unfortunately, the answer is not so straightforward. Most personality type theories hold that an individual's type is inborn and does not change. Individuals can, however, develop qualities and habits that differ from or even directly contradict the description of their type.

Character traits of successful people

The following are what I consider to be the fundamentals of good character. Miss one of these, and you will find a weak link in your character, which may be compromising the way others see you.

Integrity

Integrity is a good slogan and can sometimes seem too general a concept, but it actually gives us a new perspective on some ideal aspects of a person's character. The root of integrity is "whole" or "undivided," which is a great way to comprehend what integrity is: an undivided life. For example, you do not act one way in one setting and differently in another. Your life is full of integrity and fullness. This way of life will instill trust in your followers. Another instance of the word integrity that enlightens us is when it refers to a physical structure. Integrity refers to the strength and lack of cracks in a wall or building. The same might be said of outstanding leaders.

Sincerity

It is sometimes stated that honesty is the best policy; however, I would argue that honesty is the only policy for successful people. Consider this. Why do people obfuscate the truth? Usually for the following reasons: They are either terrified of the consequences or attempting to conceal something. In any case, a lack of honesty causes you to lose the faith of people who follow you. Even if you tell them the truth, they will lose trust in you since they know you lied to others. They begin to wonder, "If he lies to them, will he lie to me?"

I've never understood what individuals seek to achieve by lying. People eventually discover that you are not honest, which you become known for. Your reputation, on the other hand, is the foundation of your leadership. When we are honest and live truthfully in front of our followers, they can see us for who we are and make informed judgments to follow us.

Trustworthiness

People with good character are loyal. When it comes to others, they have a "stick-to-it" approach. Anyone who understands human nature understands that people fail. It is simply a matter of time, regardless of how talented someone is. Even when things are bad, a person of good character remains loyal to their friends. In good times anyone can be friends with others. People of good character stand by their friends when they are in need. This translates into being a good leader in the following way: people want to follow a leader who will support them while also allowing them to try—and fail. When we are devoted to our followers, they will be loyal to us and make every attempt to succeed on our as well as the organization's behalf. Few things strengthen the leader-follower tie more than a leader's dedication to a follower in need.

Self-sacrifice

Lee Iacocca created a legend when he vowed he'd bring Chrysler back from the verge of bankruptcy for a buck a year. This was a typical example of a leader making a sacrifice for the sake of his followers. It also demonstrated his awareness of and empathy for the common line worker. As a result, Chrysler employees rewarded him with a cult-like following as they turned Chrysler into one of the world's leading automakers.

What is it about self-sacrifice that inspires people to follow? Followers aren't afraid to put in the effort. They don't even worry if a leader makes more money or benefits from their efforts. What followers do notice is when the leader uses them for personal advantage. People with a good character do not take advantage of others. When a leader sacrifices personal gain, it communicates to followers that they are willing to come alongside them—and followers nearly uniformly appreciate this. A person of good character demonstrates that they are willing to forego personal benefit for the sake of the greater good.

Responsibility

People with a good character don't mind being held accountable. They, in fact, welcome it. Enabling others to speak to you directly about your life and conduct is the act of allowing others to have a say in your life. The harsh reality is that we have blind spots and require other people to be close to us to progress down the path of success. The requirement for accountability does not imply a lack of character. Rather, it demonstrates the presence of personality.

Followers grow bored of leaders who refuse to be held accountable. They don't mind leaders who act and make mistakes, but they do mind leaders who refuse to accept responsibility for their mistakes by holding themselves accountable. When we accept responsibility, those who follow us recognize how serious we are about keeping our affairs in order and, as a result, will do a good job leading the rest of the organization.

Self-discipline

The ability to make excellent decisions about what we will or will not do with our actions is important to who we become in terms of character. There will be several opportunities to indulge in immoral activities. Everyone faces temptations, but an excellent character understands the importance of exercising self-discipline—literal control over their decisions. When people lack self-control, they undermine their leadership. People lose respect for them and will follow them less willingly or even not at all. We can define self-control as being able to choose what we should or should not do. When we demonstrate self-control, we re-establish trust in our followers. They admire us and want to be like us.

How to improve your character habits

In interpersonal relationships, the character is important in the sense that it allows us to enhance our reputation with those who know us. Character habits are simply habits. Therefore, it is possible to change them by following some simple steps that I have identified for you.

Observe yourself

The first thing to do in building your character habits is to be honest with yourself! We often live cooped up in our own "bubble" – our own idea of ourselves. Unfortunately, our perception of ourselves is frequently incorrect - we tend to trust our publicity. Everyone considers themselves to have great character - we consider ourselves to be people of principle.

Perform a cost-benefit analysis

Being completely honest with oneself is essential. You picked up your character traits because they were helpful to you at some point in your life. However, it is very likely that some of the behaviors developed many years ago are today more costly than useful.

Choose the fuel

There is only one way to take the decisive step and change your character: You must convince yourself that the cost of your current habit outweighs the benefit of keeping it. It would be best to choose the "fuel rod" that will excite you sufficiently to develop a new habit.

Write it down

The most important thing to accomplish now is to write down your conclusions from your cost-benefit analysis. If you can't write it down and make a compelling case for why you should change, you're living in a fantasy world, and you will not modify your character habits.

Get focused

Habits, by definition, exist below the threshold of awareness. Wanting to change is one thing and actually deciding it is another. What you need to do is to focus and become aware of your habits or the patterns you follow.

Actually, there is no single method for attaining this awareness. Using your smartphone to send regular reminders to focus your attention on the habit you wish to alter works for some of you. Others find that setting aside five minutes once or twice a day to reflect on the previous few hours works wonderfully. In general, what is measured is done. One thing is sure: you must have the image of the person you want to become in the forefront of your mind.

<u>Go public</u>

Making a promise to yourself is one thing. It's totally another thing to share this commitment with people you respect and trust. This takes a lot of guts. Most people feel exposed when they publicly disclose a bad character trait. However, sharing your transformation strategy with others yields significant benefits.

Making yourself accountable, as well as people you trust and respect, greatly boosts your chances of success. You'll discover that success breeds success, and your new way of behaving will become more natural – even automatic. In a nutshell, it becomes a new habit!

<u>After six months, reevaluate</u>

The only way to truly gauge your achievement in transforming is to examine your character reputation. Return to the same people and survey them. They will most likely be delighted to give you their opinion and delighted that you want their rating.

Understanding other people

Humans are the only species capable of attempting to understand other people. Understanding people is a task that aids in the socializing process. As a result, it improves people's chances of survival in various circumstances through mutual aid.

Understanding other people allows us to observe and understand situations from multiple viewpoints as social beings. In this regard, it supports the processes involved in developing empathy and the value systems humans possess. However, just because understanding other people is an incredible skill does not imply a straightforward aim.

To truly understand people, whether you're reading your boss, coworker, or lover, you must surrender biases and break down some walls. You must be willing to let go of old, restricting assumptions, no matter how bright your intellect is.

Understanding others not only allows us to forecast how people will feel in a certain scenario but also enables us to make sense of how people will react.

How to read people

Being sensitive to other people's emotions and thoughts is a valuable talent that will aid you in navigating interpersonal relationships. Though each person is unique, we are all wired the same way on a fundamental level. Here's how to start identifying even the smallest of subtle hints.

Set a baseline

• Know the people

To truly read someone, you must first get to know them well. You'll have a greater understanding of someone's likes and dislikes, common patterns, and what is or isn't necessarily a "tell" if you get to know them personally.

Base your opinions of others on multiple interactions with them, not just one. Depending on the occasion, people may act and speak differently.

Take note of other people's habits. Do they maintain constant eye contact? When they're nervous, do their voices change? How do people communicate their dissatisfaction when they are preoccupied? This will help you understand what you should look for while attempting to read them.

• Ask open-ended questions

You are looking and listening when you read someone. What you're not doing is seizing the bull by the horns and guiding the conversation in your favor. So, ask your inquiry, and then leave. Take a seat, unwind, and enjoy the show.

Open-ended inquiries will allow them to talk more, allowing you to observe them for a longer time.

You'll be better off asking direct, pertinent inquiries. If you ask, "How's your family?" you can get a rambling, all-over-the-place response that doesn't help you measure the information you need. If you ask, "What book are you now reading?" you may be able to elicit more personal information.

• Examine their baseline for irregularities

Once you've figured out how the person behaves in everyday situations, keep an eye out for anything that doesn't fit.

If something doesn't seem to be going your way, you'll need to figure out why, at least at first. They could simply be weary, have had a dispute with their significant other, been yelled at by their supervisor, or have some minor personal issue bothering them. Before you have all the facts, don't assume it's a reflection of your connection with that person.

• Work in clusters

Seeing one indication is not enough to reach a conclusion. After all, someone may be leaning away from you simply because that chair is difficult to sit in. If you rely primarily on nonverbal cues, be sure you have three or four indicators before making assumptions.

Take cues from their words, tone, body language, and facial expressions. It may be safe to proceed once you have one from each, and they all line-up. Of course, the simplest approach to find out if you're right is to simply ask.

• Recognize your flaws

You are fallible as a mere mortal human being. When you see something beautiful, chances are you'll like it. You're more likely to believe it if it's dressed in a nicely made Italian suit. Do you think you should? No, not always.

Humans typically associate dangerous people with drunkards roaming the streets unwashed and wielding a knife. In fact, most psychopaths are pleasant and well-mannered. Though it's nearly hard to control, be aware that your subconscious is asking you to evaluate a book by its cover, which isn't always the best or most accurate thing to do.

Pay attention to body language

As we discussed earlier, body language plays a key role in how people are perceived. That's the reason why you should always pay attention to the details.

- Observe how they behave

Body language may reveal a lot about how someone is feeling, especially how comfortable they are. It could be a reflection of the topic at hand or an interpersonal issue. In the pages dedicated to body language, we talked about how to interpret the way a person moves

- Keep an eye out for brief facial expressions as well

Keep a close eye on individuals to see if any little mouth movements reveal how they are actually feeling. For example, someone may smile at you, but it could indicate that they think negatively of their lip twitches.

- Check to see whether they touch you

For example, if a person embraces you typically when they see you but doesn't this time, it could indicate that they are tense with you. Consider things like a shaky handshake, which could indicate uneasiness or anxiety.

- Take note of how far apart they are in space

The distance between you and another person might also reveal information about their mental state. For example, if a person physically distances themselves from you, it may indicate that they do not want to be vulnerable or intimate with you. It could also indicate that they are in a rush! Clusters are important once again in this case.

- Consider the cultural significance of their body language

A person's cultural background influences their body language, facial expressions, and how close they approach you. When attempting to read people, it is critical to keep these factors in mind. You don't want to get to an erroneous conclusion about someone because you saw them through a distorted lens.

Consider vocal cues

- Tone

The tone of a person's voice can reveal a lot about how they're feeling. Look for irregularities in their tone or pitch of voice. Is it possible for them to appear both happy and angry at the same time? They're most likely trying to hide something.

- Take note of the volume; are they speaking louder or softer than usual?

- Check to detect if they are hedging with their voice, frequently saying "Um" or "Uh." If this is the case, they could be frightened or lying to purchase time.

- Examine their tone to see whether it reveals an emotion that they aren't expressing directly. Do they, for example, sound sarcastic or angry? They may feel compelled to confront the situation passively. It's best to get things out in the open if this is the case.

- Responses

Short, clipped responses to inquiries may indicate that the individual is frustrated or overburdened, but extended responses may indicate that the individual is interested and content with the conversation.

- Word choice

When people say things, there is always a deeper meaning behind the words. What if someone said to you, "You're visiting another dentist?" They use the word "another" to imply, "You just visited a dentist, and it went bad — now you see another one?!"

- Spot lying

Based on what people say, it is possible to determine whether or not they are lying. Take their statements in context, and keep in mind that deciphering verbal cues is not flawless.

Using a question to answer a question allows them to spend more time making up a story.

People who use qualifiers like "to the best of my knowledge" may be dishonest.

When someone is lying, they may delete references to themselves and avoid using the word "I."

People who lie frequently utilize the present tense to refer to past events.

According to certain studies, those who use more formal speech may be lying. For example, they may not utilize contractions or titles.

When someone is guilty of something, they will occasionally use words to soften the deed. For example, instead of using the term steal, they may use the word borrow.

Chapter Four

TIME WEALTH

T ime is money. It's something you've heard a thousand times, and it makes sense. But have you ever thought about it the other way around? After all, if money is time, then time must be money. It may appear to be an unusual thought, yet the parallel holds up rather nicely. More significantly, viewing money in terms of time is one of the most effective strategies to adopt a more balanced approach to spending vs. accumulating wealth.

Whether we like it or not, we live in a culture where wealth and success are evaluated by how much money we have. We are all trained to strive for the huge house, the flashy sports cars, and the seven-digit investment account balance. This puts a terrific amount of strain on us and frequently casts doubt on our life decisions. We aren't succeeding unless we make more money.

But let me tell you something: I've worked with clients with $50,000,000 and clients with $250,000, and each experience taught me an essential lesson. Money is infinite, while time is finite. In my opinion, someone with $250,000 who uses their time exactly as they want is much wealthier than someone with $50,000,000 who has no time to enjoy it.

We become stuck in the never-ending search for more money because we don't know how much money is "enough." We make unneeded compromises in order to buy more stuff and earn more money because it's what we're supposed to do.

It's time to start focusing on time wealth rather than monetary wealth.

Time freedom

The ability to spend your valuable time in a way that is most consistent with your beliefs is referred to as time wealth. This could include spending time with family, doing a job you enjoy, volunteering, traveling, and so on.

The capacity and freedom to regulate our time should be something we all strive for. That means we're not missing our children's soccer games, we're not trapped in a job we despise, and we're not passing on significant experiences because we don't have time.

This is not a simple mindset to adopt. You'll always have acquaintances who brag about their expensive cars, or you'll see how wealthy people are idolized in the media. However, if you can get comfortable with this mindset, you will feel freer than ever before. When you begin to consider money as a tool to free up your time, it significantly impacts the financial decisions you make.

Changing spending habits

When you think about wealth in terms of time rather than money, you become a more disciplined consumer.

Assume you're thinking of making a large purchase, such as a new home. Ask yourself the following questions—

• Is this purchase going to save me time?

• Is this purchase increasing the time I spend with the most important people to me?

- Is this purchase going to necessitate a time investment? Is that something I'm okay with?

Sometimes all you need is a new house. You may have a growing family and just require additional rooms. These questions are best suited for "nice to have" purchases rather than "must-have" purchases.

Furthermore, this approach can help you become more aware of how you're currently spending your money. I know everyone despises the b-word (budget), but budgeting can be viewed as an opportunity rather than a punishment.

Budgeting raises awareness of whether or not your money is being spent according to your basic principles. What if you discovered areas where you could save money to spend more on things that would free up your time? Hiring someone to cook meals or clean your house could be a low-cost investment that significantly frees up your time.

For another example, instead of saving a lot of money for your children's school, what if you invested in family travel experiences? Maybe this is not the most cost-effective option, but it will allow you to make lasting memories for your family and teach your children about foreign cultures. This is why parents should not assume that saving for college is the smartest thing to do.

The overarching idea is that viewing wealth as time functions as a filter for your financial decisions. It protects you from purchasing items that aren't connected with your basic values.

Changing career decisions

Time wealth serves as a filter not only for your expenditures but also for your job.

Assume you have children and are offered a significantly higher-paying job that also requires a greater time commitment. When you consider wealth in terms of money rather than time, you are more inclined to accept the job because it will pay more and enhance your net worth.

When you perceive wealth as time, though, you are forced to take a much closer look at the time you are giving up. The capacity to be there and involved in their children's life is the most consistent value I have heard from parents. This time filter may stop you from wasting valuable time that cannot be replaced with more money.

What if you want to change occupations to do something you enjoy, but the salary is lower? When we have the perspective of money as the measure of success, this can be a very tough change. Taking a job that you enjoy enhances your time riches since you are now spending more of your time in ways that are consistent with your basic values.

Changing how much money you need

People who prioritize time wealth will naturally spend less than those who prioritize money wealth. According to this principle, those who spend in a disciplined manner and are inspired by minimalism always make sure that their spending conforms to their ideals.

Furthermore, "retirement" will never be a goal for you. Why would you ever want to stop maximizing your time wealth? Therefore, you will be able to generate revenue for a longer time, reducing the amount of money you will need to save to cover your living needs. This is why, if you never retire, your "traditional" financial decisions shift.

There's an easy way to figure out how much money you'll need to save before you can retire. Divide your expected annual retirement income by 4 percent, which is the maximum amount you will withdraw from your savings yearly to pay for your expenses in retirement.

Assume, for example, that your ideal lifestyle costs $100,000 per year. A standard work-life path implies that you will retire at the age of 65, which means that you will need $100,000/4% = $2,500,000 saved at that age to sustain your lifestyle.

Let's imagine you work longer because you enjoy what you do! If you continue working and earning $50,000 per year, you will only need to remove $100,000 – $50,000 = $50,000 each year from your investment account. This means you'll need to save $50,000 divided by 4% for a total of $1,250,000.

Working longer relieves you of the obligation to save a lot of money when you're younger and allows you to leave the 9-5 sooner. It also allows you to spend more time maximizing your time riches rather than your monetary wealth.

Financial freedom

Are you financially free? Did you achieve time freedom?

These are questions we must ask ourselves every day. Why is financial freedom so important? Because it allows us to reach our ultimate goal: time freedom.

Financial freedom is defined as the "capacity to existing on passive income sources gained through active revenue activities, all with the purpose of developing self-sustaining cash flow systems." This translates to starting businesses and investing in tools that make money for us while we sleep.

Consider this for a moment: we all have the same amount of time in a day: 24 hours, 1,440 minutes, and 86,400 seconds. Nobody has more time than anyone else. So, why do some people fight so much to make the most of the time we have?

It all comes down to priorities. We want to spend now rather than save for later. It's a lot easier to buy that stuff than to save money and let our hard-earned money work for us. By giving up on doing everything we can to achieve financial freedom, we fail to reach a point where we no longer have to trade our hours for pay. We voluntarily commit to a life of slavery by not saving or investing. This does not have to be the case.

We can be free. And we can enjoy what we do. We can have a life that is spent pursuing our hobbies and aspirations without worrying about where our money will come from tomorrow.

The path to financial and time freedom is straight but not simple. Discipline, courage, and tenacity are all required. The system will be difficult to learn at first, but momentum will be on your side once you get started. After all of your hard work has been completed, you will begin to see the benefits of your efforts.

The seven stages of financial freedom

I've often wondered what it would be like to have full financial freedom. Wouldn't it be wonderful to be able to live on your own terms and prioritize your time according to your needs? If you ask a layperson, they would most likely tell you that financial independence has enough money not to worry about it. While this is true in some ways, it is not the most comprehensive definition. If we aim to be financially independent, we must first comprehend all of the moving pieces.

Most people begin with a strong desire to plan and work hard for the financial freedom they have always desired. However, just like a new year's resolutions, this enthusiasm fades gradually. The main reason is that it is a time-consuming operation. To achieve financial freedom, it takes time, years in fact.

It's usually an excellent idea to divide your financial freedom journey into manageable chunks. This is more effective and performs better because it makes your goals more attainable and allows you to quickly track how far you've progressed on your path.

An important thing that has helped me personally is continually keeping track of where I was on my financial journey to financial freedom. Every month, I took a look at it. It brings me great pleasure and excitement to realize how far I've gone since deciding to pursue financial independence.

The seven stages of financial freedom are quite beneficial in instilling healthy money habits in you. These habits will follow you for the rest of your life, and you will be much better off as a result. This is a fundamental requirement for a solid money management strategy.

Dependent

If you make less than you spend, or if you do not earn at all, you are in the dependent stage. You are dependent if you rely on your parents' support or any other type of monetary support from a third party.

Solvent

If your spending is less than your income, you are at this stage. At the solvent stage, you're likely to satisfy your financial obligations, such as paying bills and other withdrawals from your account, without actively relying on anybody else.

Stable

You are in a stable phase when you have proved the ability to consistently save and spend less than your earnings and when you have paid off some of your debt. Your goal should now be to save more aggressively, first for an emergency fund and subsequently for long-term growth investments.

Security

That's when things start to heat up. You now have a solid foundation with a sizable sum of hard-earned savings. This is the time to put the money you've saved to use. What exactly do I mean? So, think about investing. Allow compound interest to work its magic. It is not a get-rich-quick scam, so you should invest money you don't want to lose in the short term and give it some time. Doing research and learning about investing is a great approach to make your money work harder for you.

Independence

At this point, you should be able to earn consistent long-term returns on your investments. Ideally, the profits on your investments should be sufficient to cover your living expenses. Dividends provided by firms and increases in business valuation are both excellent sources of income to assist you in reaching financial independence.

Freedom

Everyone aspires to achieve freedom. Being able to afford the necessities while still being able to try new things in life. Taking more calculated risks, going on vacation and having incredible experiences, engaging in a pastime you've always put off because you never had the time - now is the time. This is the time to be truly free and do whatever you've always wanted to do.

Abundance

What are you going to do with all of that money? You've reached the peak of financial achievement; now is the time to invest your money wisely. Make preparations to leave it to your beneficiaries who will appreciate it the most, or gift it to a charity to leave the world a better place by helping the less fortunate members of society.

Takeaway

Whatever stage you are at in your financial freedom journey, remember that every little amount counts. Break your goals down into smaller, more measurable goals, then celebrate your accomplishment once you've accomplished them. Remember that this journey should be enjoyable along the way. It is the journey, not the goal, that matters.

Every person is unique, and each person's journey is unique to them. Take solace in the idea that it is your personal journey - there are no right or wrong answers. Whatever works best for you is ok.

How to stop trading time for money

We were all duped. Growing up, we were sold the myth that we needed to pursue the standard career route of working 50-hour weeks to get a steady paycheck. In a nutshell, arrive to work early, stay late, and even come in on weekends, and maybe, just maybe, you'll earn a raise one day.

We hoped that if we worked "long enough," we'd be able to save enough money to retire at the age of 65. So, who the hell came up with that? When did it become a norm that we have to sacrifice our time for money?

In truth, this is one of society's most egregious falsehoods. Time is our most valuable commodity, and no amount of money can compensate for it.

Your earnings are limited by time

When you exchange time for money, your earnings will always be restricted. The first reason is that there are only 24 hours in a day to pursue money. Most of us require eight hours of sleep, two hours to commute to and from work, and two to four hours overall to cook, eat, care for our hygiene, relax, and spend time with our friends and family.

That gives us 10 to 12 hours to trade in for money. That is all there is to it. But the truth is, it doesn't matter how much your time is worth to your company: $20, $35, or $50 per hour; there is always a time limit.

Another factor to consider in the pursuit of money is that few of us can just ask for more money because we want it. We must wait years for the essential job promotion, and there is a good probability that we will not receive it at all.

The second argument for income limitations is that the more we make, the more we lose. Employee tax is the most heavily taxed type of income, and the more we make, the more tax we have to pay. This means that if someone's salary increases from $60,000 to $100,000 due to a promotion, they aren't actually earning $40,000 more.

Your time is limited

When we constantly exchange time for money throughout our lives, we have little time to pursue our passions. This might be a hobby we enjoy, giving back to the community, or creating something that has a significant impact on the globe.

Simply put, when you have a limited amount of time, you have a limited amount of influence. The question then is, how can we avoid exchanging time for money? Consider getting on the one sustainable road that will allow you to quit selling time for money. Take the following seven steps:

Modify your mindset

The first step is to adjust our beliefs. When we let go of the belief that to generate money, we must trade our time for it, our brains become more open to new options. There is no rule stating that to earn x dollars, we must labor x hours. In fact, it is more necessary to spend time "unlearning" the old than it is to spend time "learning" the new.

So, instead of trading time for money, consider trading value for money. Consider what value you can add to the lives of others and how you may give that worth. What valuable assets, skills, expertise, contacts, or ideas do you have? Recognize your strengths and competencies before going all-in.

Establish your authority and competence

We need to establish expertise around the capabilities and value we can contribute to others once we understand them. Developing expertise results in increased value creation for ourselves and others, for we can now solve problems that few people are able to.

Being regarded as an expert, on the other hand, requires time and effort, which is why gaining authority is equally crucial.

Creating authority around your expertise is what will lead people to discover it in the first place. It doesn't matter if you are the best in the world at something if no one has heard of you.

Various things contribute to authority, but the most effective include testimonials, press & media, influencer associations, and case studies. Assure individuals that you know what you're talking about. Developing expertise and authority can instantly improve the value of your time and open doors for chances to come to you.

Multiply your time

Not everyone can jump into entrepreneurship in the blink of an eye. As a result, if you're freelancing or delivering professional services for a fee, multiply your time by ten: "10x the value of your time."

Instead of working with ten clients who will pay you $2 per hour, find two who will pay you $20 per hour and drop the rest. Of course, this is easier said than done, but the rationale here is to focus on the few that produce the most results.

So you'll be working for less time for the same money, if not more. This means you'll have more time to take care of various types of wealth and become a more well-rounded person in every way.

Focus on building a new income stream

Create something that you can produce, sell and deliver without having to be present to cease selling time for money.

For example, creating an online product – such as an ebook, training program, membership program, software apps, etc. – is a fantastic approach to accomplish this. You can sell physical things online as well, but you'll need to find someone who can make and transport the product to your clients (through drop shipping).

The power of a digital product is that you can produce it once and then devote the rest of your time to selling it. Yes, you will need to improve and optimize the product, but you will do so on your own time.

This implies you may go on vacation, spend time with friends, or sleep and still profit from clients purchasing your services.

Automatize the process

Find a technique to automate and systemize everything in your firm that you can. This might include everything from how you attract consumers to how you provide your products to how you drive traffic – a wide range of areas of your business, such as your webinars, themed calendars, social media postings, Facebook advertisements, and so on.

The more you can automatize it, the more time you'll have to focus on the business rather than on it. Your time should be devoted to long-term strategy, relationship building, and business growth – the drivers that will propel your company forward.

Of course, we cannot automate and systemize every aspect of the firm. So, what are we to do?

Start outsourcing

You will definitely reach a point where your work alone will not allow you to grow your business. At that point, you will have to begin outsourcing and delegating some of your business tasks. This way, you'll gain time (we'll see how to use it in a moment) and increase your revenue.

Delegating is also a way to leverage specific skills in the various areas of your business, increasing productivity and enhancing the quality of the product or service you offer.

Develop your next business idea

You've established authority, created your product, discovered a means to automate and hire someone to help you expand your business. What comes next?

It is frequently insufficient to have a single offering on the market. The most successful companies diversify into new products or services or find a method to upsell existing clients.

Is there a product idea that one of your consumers has been bugging you about? A set of features that you can include to offer a premium-priced package? Understand what your present consumers want and devise a strategy to utilize the systems and resources you already have.

Enjoy your reward

The final stage is to reward yourself. What is the point of having extra time if we can't enjoy it? Spend time with family and friends, acquire a new skill, or travel the world. To identify the concept of having more time as a positive consequence, we must be able to picture and reward the results we have achieved.

Take some time to rest, regroup, and do more of what you enjoy. Time is only valuable if it is used wisely. When you take stock of your life, you will never regret not closing one more deal. You will be sorry for not spending more time with your partner, a friend, a child, or a parent.

Moving from active to passive income

After describing the path needed to stop trading your precious time for money, let's look at how to make a life without "traditional" work sustainable.

The income you earn through your work, profession, small business, or "investments" you must directly manage is referred to as active income. This is also known as "selling time for money." It is usually taxed at the highest possible rate.

This is active income if you are paid by the hour. Most small business income, in my opinion, is also active. If you can't go away for a year and have your income keep coming in, it's not passive. I always question myself, "Is this scalable?" as I look around my business and life. In other words, can you get more work done with the same or less effort? Active income cannot be scaled, unlike passive income!

<u>What exactly is "passive income"?</u>

Earnings from renting properties, limited partnership, or another firm in which a person is not actively participating are referred to as passive income. Passive income, like non-passive income, is normally taxable. However, the Internal Revenue Service frequently treats it differently (IRS).

My goal was to increase my passive income to the point where it exceeded my essential monthly expenses: mortgage/rent, food, utilities, and insurance. This is what I would define "financial freedom." This is when you may choose to live life on your terms, which is exactly what I desired! How can a high-earning professional replace active revenue with passive revenue?

During my business coach workshops, I teach my students that investing means putting money to work for them. I inform them that the steps to become wealthy are as follows:

1. Earn money (have a high-income business or profession)

2. Save money (have a minimal lifestyle, adopt a tax-efficient strategy)

3. Invest money (build an appropriate portfolio)

You obviously want to get to step 3 as soon as possible. You must think and act as if you are already a successful investor! If you recognize yourself in this category, the next step is to set up your accounts and portfolio so that money flows automatically into investments that grow year after year.

Beyond the theory we've just seen, I personally believe that the category of passive income should also include all those activities other than the main job that can speed our journey to financial freedom. Many people believe that passive income is about getting something for nothing, like in those 'get-rich-quick' schemes. But, in the end, it still requires some work. You simply provide the effort up front.

In reality, you may undertake some or all of the work upfront, but passive income frequently requires some additional work along the way. To keep the passive cash flowing, you may need to keep your digital product updated or your rental property well-maintained.

However, it may be a terrific method to produce revenue and create some extra financial stability for yourself and your family if you stick with it.

Passive income ideas

If you're considering developing a passive income stream, take a look at these ten ideas and learn the tricks as well as the risks connected with each plan to be successful with them.

<u>Info products</u>

One popular technique for passive income is to create an information product, such as an audio or video course or an e-book, and then sit back and watch the money stream in. Courses can be offered and sold on sites like SkillShare, Udemy, and Coursera.

You might also consider a "freemium" strategy, which entails creating a following with free content and then charging for more extensive information or for people who want to know more. This concept may be used by language teachers and stock-picking guidance, for example. The free content serves as a representation of your competence and may entice individuals wishing to advance.

Opportunity: Information products can provide a fantastic revenue stream because money may be made quickly after the initial investment of time.

Risk: Creating the product takes a great amount of effort, and it has to be amazing in order to make good money from it. There is no place for garbage out there.

To get good results, you must establish a strong platform, advertise your items, and prepare for future items. Creating additional fantastic products is the best method to market an existing product. Once you learned the business model, you can build an excellent income stream.

<u>Rentals</u>

Typically, creating passive income in real estate entails purchasing a property and renting it out to renters. Managing rental properties can be a lucrative source of income. On the other hand, being a landlord is not a completely passive source of income and takes regular effort. Tenants will expect you to maintain and update your home regularly. You must also devote some time to investigating your property possibilities and advertising your available space.

I will now briefly summarize the necessary steps to start this type of business.

Research

Before you ever consider purchasing a rental property, you should conduct extensive research in your local area. First, use a real estate database to see what rental units are currently available in your region. This will give you a decent indication of how much rent you can realistically charge. Keep in mind that your home's amenities, location, and size will all have an impact on how much rent you can charge.

You'll also need to spend time understanding the laws that apply to landlords. The majority of states have many housing rules that govern what a landlord can and cannot do. Violations of your state's housing regulations might result in serious legal consequences.

Do the math

After you've done your homework on the local real estate market and housing laws, it's time to pick a home. Choose a cheap house in a location where you can demand enough rent to repay the mortgage if one is required. Investigate the typical cost of utilities in the area where you intend to purchase a home. If you intend to purchase the house with a mortgage loan, you should also look at current interest rates.

Once you've found the ideal house, sit down and figure out how much rent you'll need to charge to make a profit.

Secure a mortgage

If you do not like to pay for your rental property in cash, you must obtain a mortgage. A government-backed loan cannot be used to purchase a rental property. Instead, you must meet the conditions of your lender for a traditional investment property loan. These loans may be more difficult to obtain, particularly if you have never handled a rental property previously.

Rent your space

When you've received your home loan and your property is ready to sell, it's time to begin promoting. Advertise your unit on real estate database websites like Apartments.com and local online markets like Facebook marketplace or Craigslist. Make it clear how interested parties can contact you or apply for the spot.

When you receive applications, give each one due consideration. Be choosy about your tenants and wait for a few applications before making a decision. Some states have very strict tenant rights legislation, so you should be very careful about who you rent to. However, you must also ensure that you are not influencing your selection with preconceptions or previous assumptions.

The only thing left to do now that your renters have moved in is to be a wonderful landlord! Provide your tenants with clear rent expectations, and answer maintenance requests as soon as possible. Tenants are more inclined to respect your space if you respect them.

Dividend stocks

Shareholders in corporations with dividend-paying stocks receive a payout from the company regularly. Companies pay cash dividends out of their profits on a regular basis, and all you have to do is own the stock. Dividends are paid per share; therefore, the more shares you own, the higher your dividend. Owning dividend-yielding stocks can be one of the most passive ways to make money because the income is not connected to any action other than the initial financial investment. The funds will be put directly into your brokerage account.

The tough aspect is picking the correct stocks.

Companies that pay out a large dividend, for example, may be unable to maintain it. Too many newcomers enter the market without first properly researching the company issuing the stock. You must research each company's website and be confident in their financial statements, and you must spend at least two weeks studying each company.

However, there are ways to invest in dividend-paying stocks without spending a lot of time researching. How is it possible? Just using exchange-traded funds or ETFs. ETFs are investment vehicles that hold assets such as equities, commodities, and bonds but trade similarly to stocks. ETFs also diversify your assets, so if a company reduces its dividend, it has little effect on the ETF's price or income.

ETFs are an excellent choice for beginners since they are simple to comprehend, extremely liquid, and inexpensive, with significantly higher potential returns due to reduced costs than mutual funds.

Risk: stocks or ETFs can fall precipitously in a short time, particularly during times of uncertainty, such as in 2020, when the Covid-19 crisis startled financial markets. Economic stress can also cause some corporations to completely cut their payouts, but diversified funds may fare better.

REITs

A real estate investment trust is a fancy title for a company that controls and manages real estate. REITs have a unique legal structure that allows them to pay minimal or no corporate income tax if they distribute the majority of their earnings to shareholders.

Opportunity: REITs can be purchased on the stock market like any other firm or dividend stock. You will earn whatever dividends the REIT pays out, and the best REITs have a track record of increasing their payouts on an annual basis, so you might have a growing source of income over time. Individual REITs, like dividend stocks, can be riskier than holding an ETF that includes dozens of REIT firms. A fund provides rapid diversification and is typically far safer than purchasing individual equities - and you'll still get a decent reward.

Risk: Just with dividend stocks, you'll need to be able to identify the solid REITs, which means you'll need to evaluate each business you're considering buying – a time-consuming process. The price of this stock, like any other, might move a lot in the near term. And, while it is a passive pastime, you might lose a lot of money if you don't know what you're doing.

Even dividends distributed by REITs are also not immune to economic downturns. If the REIT does not earn enough money, it will most likely have to reduce or discontinue its dividend. As a result, your passive income may suffer just when you need it the most.

Retail products flipping

Use popular online marketplaces such as Amazon or eBay to sell things that you find out at low costs elsewhere. You will arbitrage the difference between your purchase and selling prices, and you may be able to establish a following of people who follow your trades.

Opportunity: You will profit from price discrepancies between what you can find and what the common consumer can find. This could be most effective if you have a contact who can assist you in obtaining inexpensive products that few other people can find. Alternatively, you may be able to uncover valuable items that others have just overlooked.

Risk: While internet sales can occur at any moment, making this technique passive, you will undoubtedly have to work hard to find a reputable supply of merchandise. You'll need to be well-versed in the market to avoid paying too much. You'll also need to invest money in all of your products until they sell, so you'll need a steady supply of funds. Otherwise, you can end up with things that no one wants or whose prices must be dramatically reduced in order to sell.

<u>Affiliate marketing</u>

Influencers, website owners or bloggers use affiliate marketing to promote a third-party product by providing a link to the product on their social media accounts or website. Amazon is the most well-known affiliate partner, while eBay, ShareASale, and Awin are other big names. In addition, Instagram and TikTok have grown into massive platforms for individuals trying to build a following and market their business.

You may also consider building an email list to attract attention to your blog or direct readers to items and services they might be interested in.

Opportunity: The site owner earns a commission when a visitor clicks on the link and purchases from the third-party affiliate. The commission may range from 3 to 10 percent, implying that large traffic to your site will be required to produce high income. However, if you can increase your following or specialize in a more profitable field (such as software, fitness, or financial services), you may be able to make some real money.

Affiliate marketing is considered passive since you can earn money simply by placing a link to your website or social media account.

Obviously, if you can't get readers to click on the link and buy something, you won't make any money.

Risk: If you're just getting started, it will take some time to produce content and increase traffic. It can take a long time to create a following, and you'll need to find the ideal recipe for drawing that audience, which may take some time. Worse, once you've used all of your efforts, your audience may abandon you in favor of the next trendy influencer or social media site.

Bond laddering

Bond laddering is an investing technique that entails purchasing bonds with varying maturity dates so that the investor can respond to changes in interest rates reasonably fast. It lowers the risk of reinvestment associated with rolling over maturing bonds into equivalent fixed income products all at once.

A bond ladder is a traditional passive investment that has long appealed to retirees and near-retirees. You can sit back and receive interest payments, and when the bond matures, you "extend the ladder," trying to roll the principal into a different set of bonds. For example, you could begin with 1/3/5/7-year bonds.

When the first bond expires in a year, you will have bonds maturing in two, four, and six years. The profits from the recently matured bond can be used to purchase another one-year bond or to roll out to a longer duration bond, such as an eight-year bond.

Risk: A bond ladder reduces one of the biggest hazards of purchasing bonds: the risk that when your bond matures, you will have to purchase a new bond at a time when interest rates may be unfavorable.

Bonds also carry additional risks. For example, while the federal government guarantees treasury bonds, corporate bonds are not, which means you could lose all the money you invested if the company fails. Furthermore, if overall interest rates rise, the value of your bonds may fall. And you'll want to hold a variety of bonds to diversify your risk and reduce the possibility of a single bond negatively impacting your total portfolio.

Because of these worries, many investors turn to bond ETFs, which provide a diversified portfolio of bonds that can be set up in a ladder, removing the danger of a single bond undermining your profits.

Selling stock videos

While stock photography has been a source of money for a long time and is thus a pretty saturated market, stock videography is different. Brands are increasingly looking for stock videos to enhance their social, TV, and digital campaigns, yet the stock video industry has significant gaps. There has never been a better moment to sell stock footage.

Of course, selling stock footage is more complicated than simply uploading a few movies and calling it a day. Each platform necessitates a distinct approach, and the kind of video also provides its own set of legal constraints.

Opportunity: Exploring the web, you can find a wide selection of platforms where creators can sell stock footage, including Getty and iStock (which belong to the same group), Pond5, Shutterstock, Vimeo, and VideoHive. While all platforms give contributors a similar upload experience, some offer better rates than others. So again, it's a matter of doing some preliminary research to determine which option best suits your needs.

Some agencies require content exclusivity, but as general advice, it is better to publish your work on as many platforms as possible so as to reach every customer niche.

Food, travel, people, and lifestyle are the most popular stock footage categories on sites like Getty. High-quality drone footage is also becoming more popular, but it's best to make sure you have all the permits before selling footage made with a drone.

Of course, you can't sell just any kind of footage. Generally speaking, we can distinguish two main categories: commercial or editorial licensing. The former is used to sell something; the latter describes events or tells stories. Commercial footage pays better but also has stricter clauses; agencies require releases for models and, in many cases, for any properties that appear in the footage (buildings, monuments, etc.).

Risk: This is a growing but already very competitive market. In order to be successful, it is necessary to have high-level equipment (even if today prices have dropped a lot) and photographic skills. You can't just wing it.

Airbnb

This basic method converts space that you aren't using into a money-making opportunity. If you're going away for the summer and you need to be out of town for a long, or simply want to travel, think about renting out your apartment while you're gone. In my book *"The New Side Hustle Handbook,"* I explain this type of business in detail and provide some smart tricks to get the most out of it.

Opportunity: You may offer your room on Airbnb and set your rental terms. You'll get paid for your efforts with little extra work, especially if you're renting to a tenant who will be around for a few months.

Risk: There isn't much financial risk here, but allowing strangers to stay in your home is an unusual risk for most passive investments. Tenants may deface or even ruin your property, or they may steal valuable objects. However, Airbnb luckily provides basic insurance to cover some of these risks.

Peer to peer lending

Peer-to-peer (P2P) lending allows people to acquire loans directly from other people, bypassing the financial institution as a middleman. Instead of going to a bank and applying for a loan, the borrower uses platforms that connect them to investors like you. This enables you to lend money to an individual or a business in exchange for regular monthly payments.

Instead of the meager returns of a savings account, you obtain great interest rates in exchange for the risk you take with unsecured loans to unknown persons. In most cases, this is accomplished through an online peer-to-peer lending service that connects lenders and borrowers. Furthermore, these firms typically vet the borrower to protect lenders.

To get the most bang for your money, find an online platform that you can rely on and that provides the finest results.

Check out Prosper and LendingClub, two peer-to-peer lending networks with hundreds of live offers available at all times. Solo Funds is a community-driven platform that also piqued our interest. Finally, Mainvest is an intriguing alternative at the heart of the pandemic recovery, providing the option to lend to small businesses around the country and be reimbursed with a portion of future earnings.

The lender can place their P2P lending wherever, from healthcare finance to personal debt consolidation. That gives you more control over your portfolio and makes it easier to diversify.

Opportunity: As a lender, you earn money by collecting interest payments on loans. However, because the loan is unsecured, there is a chance of default, which means you could wind up with nothing.

To reduce that danger, you must do two things:

First, diversify your portfolio by investing small sums across various loans (minimum loan investment usually is $25), and second, analyze past data on prospective borrowers to make well-informed decisions.

Risk: Because mastering the parameters of P2P lending takes time, it is not 100% passive. You will want to properly assess your prospective borrowers, and because you are investing in several loans, you have to pay full attention to payments received. If you want to build an income, you should reinvest all of your interest earnings.

Best passive income apps

In the digital age, creating passive income cannot ignore the earning opportunities offered by many apps. I have selected for you the ten best mobile apps available on the market that can allow you to earn extra income without having to invest a lot of time.

Fundrise

This app enables you to invest in real estate projects with little to no effort on your side – and is an ideal choice if you want to create a new source of income. You will require an initial investment to start building a new portfolio. Fundrise claims to have minimal costs because of proprietary software that works hard to save you money, allowing you to generate higher returns. There are various account levels accessible, and you can select the type of investment strategy that best suits your objectives.

Key points:

• Investments in real estate
• Low fees
• More strategies available
Public.com

Through this app, you can invest in various companies. It offers themed packages in which you can invest in multiple firms that share a common subject. Women entrepreneurs and environmentally responsible businesses are two examples of such subjects. Still, you also have the opportunity to connect - through social media - with other investors who are going through the same journey as you.

If you want to invest in large corporations but don't want to spend the money to acquire a whole stock, you can acquire fractional shares.

Key points:

- Interaction with experienced traders
- Minimum capital required to start
- Themes for diversified investing

InBoxDollars

This app provides users with cashback on purchases as well as cash for doing regular activities that you're likely to undertake anyhow. Watching television, doing online surveys, and exploring the web are all acceptable methods for rewarding customers with cash offers.

A mobile app is available to let you generate money while you're out (with a bonus just for signing up).

Key points:

- Shopping cashback
- Earn money for daily activities
- Signup bonus

TrimApp

Trim examines your spending and proposes methods to save money by cutting back on expenditures. It operates in the background and requires no interaction from you.

It is likewise free to use, but it gets a cut of any savings you achieve. Trim makes it incredibly simple to save money, and while it isn't income, it is still extra money in your pocket.

Key points:

- Completely transparent way to help you save money
- No paid subscription needed
- You "pay" only with a percentage of your savings

Drop App

This app helps users to earn points for a wide range of purchases, from your morning coffee to a late-night takeaway order after a long working day. Every transaction made through the website earns you points that can be redeemed at various retailers and apps, including Uber, Netflix, Amazon, and Starbucks.

Key points:

- Earning points is simple
- Many options to redeem points

Paribus

Paribus synchronizes with your email to look for any recent online transactions you may have made. It will then compare the amount you paid to current prices and, if possible, assist you in negotiating a refund. If you are successful, the price difference will be mailed to you. They monitor over 25 of the world's largest retailers.

Key points:

- Determines if you are entitled to a refund
- Can receive reimbursement for late deliveries

Acorns

Acorns is a micro-savings and micro-investment app. It automatically rounds up your purchases to the nearest dollar. A Robo-advisor saves the additional money and invests it. When you make a purchase from any of the 350+ partner retailers, you will also receive a bonus investment.

Key points:

- Your spare change is saved and invested
- Bonus cash back on investments
- 256-bit encryption ensures maximum security

Rakuten

Rakuten is a Japanese company offering up to 40% cash back on purchases at over 2,500 stores. To get cash back on eligible purchases, you have only to click Rakuten's link to the store of your choice. There is a $10 sign-up bonus, one of the highest offered by such programs, and you can be paid via PayPal.

Key points:

- Cash back of up to 40%
- There are almost 2,500 stores to select from
- Sign-up bonus of $10

Neighbor

This app allows you to rent out any extra storage space you may have to neighbors. As a P2P storage platform, the app saves users up to 50% on storage space rentals while also being safer since they offer a good guarantee for both the host and the renter. Payments are secure and automatic, and app users are verified for further security.

Key points:

- Rent out storage space
- Guarantees for both the host and the tenant
- Renting out your garage can earn you more than $1,000

Robinhood

Robinhood is an investment app that aims to provide everyone with the tools needed to create an investment portfolio. There is no account minimum and no fees for the basic entry-level account. The app has a user-friendly design and lets you invest in many ways, including ETFs, cryptocurrencies, and equities traded on the NYSE.

Key points:

- Easy to use interface
- The basic account is completely free
- There is no account minimum

Chapter Five

PHYSICAL WEALTH

L et's face it, without the energy of a healthy body, it's nearly impossible to build and maintain the other types of wealth. The famous saying "Health is Wealth" reflects this truth.

We can imagine physical wealth as the glue that holds all other types of wealth together. We cannot obtain any other form of riches, or at least not in a prudent and long-term manner, unless our bodies are in good health and physical vitality.

Most people do not realize that good health is the foundation of every other human activity. They, therefore, neglect to devote the necessary attention to their bodies and minds, underestimating the importance of this effort in achieving the other types of wealth.

Let's see how to master the fundamentals of physical wealth!

Healthy nutrition

Good nutrition does not imply imposing harsh restrictions, remaining impossibly thin, or depriving yourself of the things you enjoy. It's more about feeling fantastic, having more energy, increasing your health, and enhancing your mood.

Eating healthy does not have to be difficult. You're not alone if you're feeling overwhelmed by all of the contradicting nutrition and diet advice out there. It appears that for every expert who says a certain cuisine is excellent for you, there is another who says the exact opposite. While certain meals or minerals have been demonstrated to positively affect mood, your overall dietary pattern is most significant. When feasible, replace processed foods with whole foods as the foundation of a balanced diet. Eating food as close to its natural state as possible can significantly impact how you think, look, and feel.

By following these basic guidelines, you will be able to cut through the confusion and learn how to create—and keep to—a delightful, varied, and healthy diet that is as beneficial for your mind as it is for your body.

The basics of healthy eating

While some diet plans may suggest differently, we all require a balanced diet of protein, fat, carbohydrates, fiber, vitamins, and minerals to maintain a healthy body. You do not need to remove certain food groups from your diet; instead, choose the healthiest selections from each group.

Protein

Protein provides the energy you need to get up and go—and keep going—while also supporting mood and cognitive function. Too much protein can be dangerous to people with kidney illness, but a new study reveals that many of us, especially as we age, require extra high-quality protein. That doesn't mean you should consume more animal products; eating a mix of plant-based protein sources each day helps ensure your body gets all of the essential protein it requires.

Fat

Not all fat is created equal. While poor fats can derail your diet and put you at risk for certain diseases, good fats safeguard your brain and heart. In reality, healthy fats, such as omega-3 fatty acids, are essential for your physical and emotional well-being. Increasing the amount of good fat in your diet can enhance your mood, improve your health, and even help you lose weight.

Fiber

Fiber is a component of plant-based meals that the body cannot digest. It goes through the stomach undigested, preserving your digestive tract clean and healthy, relaxing bowel movements, and washing away cholesterol and dangerous carcinogens. Eating high-fiber meals (fruits, vegetables, grains, nuts, and beans) can help you keep regular and lessen your risk of heart disease, stroke, and diabetes. It can also help you lose weight and make your skin look good.

Calcium

A diet low in calcium can cause anxiety, melancholy, and sleep problems, in addition to osteoporosis. Whatever your age or gender, it's essential to incorporate calcium-rich foods in your diet, minimize calcium-depleting foods, and obtain adequate magnesium, D, and K to help calcium do its work.

Carbohydrates

They are one of your body's primary energy sources. However, the majority of your carbohydrate intake should come from complex, unrefined carbs (vegetables, whole grains, fruit) rather than sweets and processed carbs. Cutting less on white bread, pastries, carbs, and sugar will help you avoid blood sugar spikes, mood and energy swings, and fat buildup, especially around your midsection.

Switching to a healthy diet

When you decide to adopt a healthier diet, it doesn't have to be all or nothing. You don't have to be perfect, you don't have to deprive yourself of the foods or snacks that you enjoy, and you don't have to change everything all at once—doing so generally results in cheating or abandoning your new eating plan.

Making a few tiny modifications at a time is a preferable approach. Maintaining modest goals will help you achieve more in the long run without feeling deprived or overwhelmed by a drastic diet change. Consider arranging a healthy diet as a series of modest, attainable actions, such as include a salad in your meal once a day. As your tiny modifications become habitual, you can gradually introduce healthier options.

Preparing yourself for success

Eating a more nutritious diet does not have to be difficult. To increase your chances of success, keep things simple. Instead of being overly concerned with calorie counts, consider your food in terms of color, variety, and freshness. When feasible, avoid packaged and processed foods in favor of more fresh ingredients.

Make more of your own food. Cooking more meals at home can help you take control of what you eat and better monitor what exactly goes into your food. You'll consume fewer calories and avoid the chemical additives, added sugar, and unhealthy fats found in packaged and takeaway foods, which can make you fatigued, bloated, and irritated, as well as increase symptoms of depression, stress, and anxiety.

Make the necessary modifications

When reducing the number of bad foods in your diet, it is critical to replace them with healthy alternatives. Replacing hazardous trans fats with beneficial fats (for example, swapping fried chicken for grilled salmon) will absolutely improve your health.

Examine the labels

It is critical to be aware of what is in your food because manufacturers frequently conceal substantial amounts of sugar or bad fats in packaged food, even those labeled as healthy.

Consider how you feel after you eat

This will aid in the development of healthy new habits and tastes. The better you feel after a meal, the healthier the food you eat. The more unhealthy food you eat, the more likely you feel bloated, sick, or exhausted.

Drink a lot of water

Water cleanses our systems of waste and poisons, but many of us go through life dehydrated, resulting in lethargy, poor energy, and headaches. Because it is typical to confuse thirst for hunger, staying hydrated will also help you make healthier eating choices.

Why moderation is important

What exactly is moderation? In essence, it is consuming only what your body requires. At the end of a meal, you should feel satiated but not stuffed. Many of us associate moderation with eating less than we do currently. But that doesn't imply you have to give up your favorite foods. If you pair it with a healthy lunch and supper, eating bacon for breakfast could be considered moderation once a week, but not if you follow it with a box of donuts and a sausage pizza.

No foods are "off-limits"

When some foods are prohibited, it is normal to crave them much more and feel like a failure if you give in to temptation. Begin by limiting the number of harmful meals you eat and consuming them less frequently. As you minimize your intake of unhealthy foods, you may discover that you crave them less or regard them as merely infrequent treats.

Consider smaller portions

Recently, serving sizes have exploded. When dining out, order a starter instead of an entree, split a dish with a companion, and avoid ordering anything supersized. Visual cues can help with portion proportions at home. A portion of meat, fish, or chicken should be approximately the size of a deck of cards, and half a cup of mashed potato, rice, or pasta should be approximately the size of a standard light bulb.

You can fool your brain into believing you're eating a larger piece by serving your meals on smaller plates or in bowls. If you aren't full after a meal, add more leafy greens or finish with fruit.

No hurry!

Slow down and consider food as nourishment rather than something to gulp down in between meetings or on the way to pick up the kids. It takes your brain a few minutes to signal your body that it has had enough food, so eat carefully and stop eating before you feel full.

Eat with others

Eating alone, especially watching TV or in front of your computer, frequently results in mindless overeating. So whenever possible, try to share lunch or dinner time with someone. Both your stomach and your mind will benefit.

Reduce snack foods at home

Take caution with the foods you keep on hand. When you keep unhealthy snacks and treats on hand, it is more difficult to eat in moderation. Instead, surround yourself with healthy options, and when you're ready to treat yourself, go out and buy it.

Manage your emotional eating

We don't always eat to fulfill our hunger. Instead, many of us resort to food to relieve stress or cope with negative emotions like melancholy, loneliness, or boredom. However, by learning healthy ways to manage stress and emotions, you may recover control over your eating habits and emotions.

More fruits and vegetables!

Fruits and vegetables are low in calories but high in nutrients, including minerals, vitamins, antioxidants, and fiber. Focus on eating at least five servings of fruit and vegetables every day to naturally fill you full and help you cut back on bad foods. A serving is half a cup of raw fruit or vegetables, such as a small banana or apple. Most of us need to consume twice as much as we do now.

To increase your intake, do the following:

• Boost the antioxidant content of your favorite breakfast cereal with berries

• For dessert, eat a mix of sweet fruit— pineapple, mangos, oranges, and grapes

• When possible, exchange your usual pasta or pizza with fresh and colorful salads

• Snack on veggies like cherry tomatoes, carrots, or peppers with a spicy hummus dip instead of packaged snacks.

Make your vegetables tasty

While basic salads and steamed vegetables can easily get boring, there are numerous ways to spice up your vegetable dishes.

• More color

Brighter, deeper-colored veggies not only have higher amounts of vitamins, minerals, and antioxidants, but they can also modify the flavor of meals and make them more visually appealing. Fresh or sundried tomatoes, caramelized carrots or beets, roasted red cabbage wedges, yellow squash, or sweet, colorful peppers can all be used to add color.

- Spice up your green salads

Experiment with foods other than lettuce. Nutrient-dense foods include spinach, mustard greens, arugula, kale, broccoli, and Chinese cabbage. Try spreading olive oil on your salad greens, adding a spicy dressing, or sprinkling with nut slices, a little bacon, parmesan chickpeas, or goat cheese to enhance flavor.

- Don't forget the sweetness

Carrots, sweet potatoes, beets, yams, bell peppers, onions, and squash are naturally sweet veggies that satisfy your sweet tooth while decreasing your cravings for extra sugar. For a delicious sweet kick, add them to stews, soups, or pasta sauces.

- New cooking styles

Broccoli, asparagus, green beans, and Brussels sprouts can all be prepared in unique ways. Roast, grill, or pan-fry these healthful sides with garlic, chili flakes, shallots, onions, or mushrooms instead of just steaming or boiling them. Alternatively, marinate them in lime juice or tart lemon before cooking.

Healthy sleep

Sleep is a vital function that helps your mind and body to replenish, allowing you to wake up refreshed and rested. A good night's sleep also helps the body stay healthy and avoid ailments. The brain cannot function correctly if it does not get adequate sleep. This has the potential to hinder your ability to concentrate, think effectively, and process memories.

Most adults require between seven and nine hours of sleep per night. Children and teenagers require significantly more sleep, especially if they are under the age of five. Work schedules, day-to-day stressors, a noisy bedroom environment, and medical issues can all interfere with getting enough sleep. A balanced diet and excellent living choices can help maintain an adequate quantity of sleep each night, but a chronic lack of sleep may be the first indicator of a sleep disorder in some people.

Top benefits of good night's sleep

Poor sleep at night can make you irritable the following day. And, over time, sleep deprivation can affect more than just your morning mood. According to studies, getting enough regular sleep might help you improve the quality of your life both physically and mentally. Here are some good reasons to take care of your night's sleep.

Enhancing your brain functions

When you're sleep-deprived, you'll likely have difficulty retaining and remember things. It happens because sleep plays an important role in both memory and learning. It's difficult to focus and absorb new knowledge when you don't get enough sleep. In addition, your brain does not have enough time to correctly store memories so that you can access them later.

Improving body weight control

According to research, people who sleep fewer hours per night seem to be more likely to become overweight or obese. A lack of sleep is known to disrupt the balance of hormones in the body that control appetite.

Sleep deprivation has been shown to affect the hormones ghrelin and leptin, which regulate hunger. If you want to maintain or reduce weight, don't forget that getting enough sleep each night is fundamental.

In addition, some recent research indicates that sleeping well at night is linked with lower calorie consumption during the day.

Reducing inflammation

There is a connection between obtaining enough sleep and lowering inflammation in the body. Inflammation is heightened as a result of increased stress hormones induced by a lack of sleep.

A new study, for example, reveals a relation between sleep deprivation and inflammatory bowel illnesses, which impact the gastrointestinal tract. In addition, this study found that sleep deprivation can lead to these diseases and that these diseases, in turn, can lead to sleep deprivation.

Boosting mood

Another activity your brain does while sleeping is processing emotions. Your mind requires this time to recognize and respond appropriately. When you cut it short, you are more likely to have negative emotional reactions and fewer pleasant ones.

A chronic lack of sleep can also increase the likelihood of developing a mental condition. For example, according to one major study, you are five times more likely to acquire depression if you suffer insomnia. In addition, your chances of developing anxiety or panic disorders are significantly higher.

A good night's sleep can help you reset your day, enhance your attitude on life, and be better prepared to face problems.

Better sport performances

Sleep deprivation may not affect you as much if your sport involves fast spurts of energy, such as boxing or bodybuilding, as it does in endurance sports such as swimming, running, and biking. However, you are not doing yourself any favor.

Lack of sleep depletes your energy and time for muscle regeneration and reduces your motivation, which propels you to the finish line.

Instead, you'll encounter a more difficult mental and physical struggle, as well as slower reaction times.

Proper rest prepares you for peak performance.

Regularize blood sugar

The level of glucose in your blood decreases during the deep, slow-wave phase of your sleep cycle. Because there isn't enough time in this deepest stage, you don't get the break to allow a reset, similar to leaving the volume turned up. As a result, your body will have a more difficult time responding to the needs of your cells and blood sugar levels.

Allowing yourself to reach and maintain this deep sleep reduces your chances of developing type 2 diabetes.

Reducing the risk of cancer

Did you know that those who work the night shift are more likely to develop breast and colon cancer? This is because light exposure, according to researchers, lowers melatonin levels. Melatonin, a hormone that determines the sleep-wake cycle, is regarded to be anti-cancer because it appears to inhibit tumor growth.

To help your body develop melatonin, keep your bedroom dark and avoid using electronic devices before sleeping.

Fighting stress

When you don't get enough sleep, your body slips into a condition of tension. As a result, the body's systems are activated, resulting in increased blood pressure and the generation of stress hormones. High blood pressure increases your chance of a heart attack or stroke, and stress hormones make it difficult to sleep. Learn relaxing techniques to help you sleep better and fall asleep sooner.

Healthy sleep tips

It is widely acknowledged that sleep is critical to our physical and mental wellbeing. Despite this, a disturbing amount of people are consistently deprived of decent sleep and are noticeably drowsy during the day.

Even though there are several causes and types of sleeping issues, expert consensus leads to a few basic strategies that promote more peaceful sleep.

Trying to adopt all of these tactics might be overwhelming for many people. But keep in mind that it's not an all-or-nothing situation; you can start with tiny modifications and gradually work your way up to healthy sleep habits, often known as sleep hygiene.

We've divided these sleep hygiene improvements into four categories to make them more approachable: Each area contains specific measures that you may take to help you go asleep, stay asleep, and wake up rested.

Set up a sleep-friendly bedroom

Making your bedroom a place of relaxation and comfort is an important piece of advice for falling asleep quickly and comfortably. Though it may appear simple, it is frequently disregarded, adding to difficulty falling asleep and sleeping through the night.

Focus on optimizing comfort and avoiding distractions while creating your sleeping environment, including the following suggestions:

- Invest in mattress and pillow

A good mattress is essential for ensuring that you are comfortable enough to relax. In conjunction with your pillow, it also ensures that your spine receives adequate support to avoid aches and pains.

- Select high-quality bedding

Your sheets and blankets play an important role in making your bed seem pleasant. Look for bedding that is soft to the touch and will help you maintain a comfortable temperature while sleeping.

- Avoid excessive light exposure

Excessive light exposure might disrupt your sleep and circadian cycle. However, light can be blocked and prevented from interfering with your sleep by using blackout curtains over your windows or a sleep mask over your eyes.

- Cultivate quiet and peace

If you want to create an environment favorable to quality sleep, one of the main concerns should be keeping noise to a minimum. If you cannot eliminate surrounding noise sources, attempt drowning them out with a fan or white noise machine. Earplugs or headphones are another alternatives for blocking out harsh sounds while you sleep.

- Find a comfortable temperature

You must always be careful that the temperature of your bedroom is appropriate, for a too hot or a too cold atmosphere can be one of the main sources of disturbance to your sleep. Of course, the appropriate temperature varies depending on the individual, but most studies suggest sleeping in a cooler room with a temperature of around 65 degrees.

- Enjoy relaxing aromas

A mild perfume that you find relaxing will help you go asleep. Essential oils with natural smells, like lavender, can bring a relaxing and refreshing scent to your bedroom.

Improve your sleep schedule

Taking charge of your daily sleep pattern is a significant step toward improved sleep. Try applying the following four ways to start harnessing your schedule for your benefit:

- Set a regular wake uptime

It is almost impossible for your body to adapt to a healthy sleep habit if you continuously wake up at different times. Set a wake-up time and stick to it, even on weekends and other days when you might be tempted to sleep in.

- Value the time you sleep

If you want to ensure that you obtain the required amount of sleep each night, you must arrange that time. Working backward from your predetermined wake-up time, determine a target bedtime. Then, allow yourself extra time before bedtime to wind down and prepare for sleep whenever feasible.

- Use caution with napping

A very serious threat to the quality of your night's sleep is naps. If you nap for too long or too late in the day, it might disrupt your sleep rhythm and make it difficult to fall asleep when you need to. The optimal time to nap is just after lunch, in the early afternoon, and the ideal nap length is approximately 20 minutes.

- Adjust your sleep schedule gradually

When changing your sleep schedule, it's preferable to do so gradually and with a maximum variation of 1-2 hours every night6. This allows your body to adjust to the changes, making it easier to stick to your new routine.

Create a bedtime routine

It's normal to believe that if you have trouble falling asleep, the problem begins when you lie down in bed. But, in actuality, the period leading up to night is critical in preparing you to fall asleep fast and easily.

Poor pre-bedtime routines are a key cause of insomnia and other sleep issues. Changing these habits takes time, but the effort can pay off by making you more relaxed and ready to sleep when evening arrives.

As far as possible, strive to establish a consistent schedule that you adhere to each night because it reinforces healthy behaviors and signals to the mind and body that bedtime is approaching. Include the following three suggestions as part of your routine:

• Relax for at least 30 minutes

When you are at peace, it is much easier to fall asleep. Quiet reading, low-impact stretching, listening to calming music, and relaxation techniques are examples of techniques for preparing for sleep.

• Dim the lights

Avoiding strong light will assist your transition to nighttime and contribute to your body's creation of melatonin, a sleep-promoting hormone.

• Turn off displays

Tablets, cell phones, and laptop computers can keep your brain wired, making it difficult to relax completely. The light from these devices can also reduce your natural melatonin production. Try to unplug for 30 minutes or more before going to bed, if possible.

Develop sleep-friendly habits

Setting the stage for a good night's sleep takes all day. However, a few simple steps you can take during the day will help you sleep better at night.

• Enjoy daylight

Light exposure regulates our internal rhythms. Sunlight has the most powerful effect, so attempt to acquire some by going outside or opening windows or blinds to let in some natural light. Getting some sunlight early in the day can help to reset your circadian rhythm. If natural light is not an option, consult your doctor about using a light treatment box.

- Exercise regularly

Daily exercise has numerous health benefits, and the changes it causes in energy usage and body temperature can support sound sleep. However, most experts advise against engaging in strenuous exercise close to bedtime since it may impair your body's capacity to relax effectively before sleeping.

- Reduce caffeine

Caffeinated beverages, such as coffee, tea, and sodas, are among the most popular beverages worldwide. Some people are tempted to utilize caffeine's energy shock to overcome daytime tiredness, but this method is not sustainable and can lead to long-term sleep deprivation. To avoid this, limit your coffee intake and avoid it later in the day when it might be a barrier to going asleep.

- Control alcohol intake

Because alcohol can cause drowsiness, some people think it's not so bad to enjoy a nightcap before bed. Unfortunately, alcohol interacts with the brain in ways that can reduce the quality of sleep; therefore, it is recommended to avoid alcohol in the hours leading up to bedtime.

- Dine early

It can be difficult to fall asleep if your body is still digesting a large meal. To reduce food-related sleep interruptions to a minimum, avoid late dinners and limit fatty or spicy foods. If you need a snack in the evening, go for something light and healthy.

- Don't smoke

Smoking, including secondhand smoke, has been linked to various sleeping issues, including trouble falling asleep and interrupted sleep.

- The bed is made for sleeping (and intimate moments) only

If you have a comfy bed, you may be tempted to spend time on it while doing various things, but this can pose problems at sleep. If you want a great mental connection between your bed and sleep, limit your actions in your bed to sleep and amorous congress!

- If You Can't Get To Sleep

It may be difficult to fall asleep when you first go into bed or when you wake up in the middle of the night. These suggestions will assist you in determining what to do if you are unable to sleep:

<u>If you struggle to sleep</u>

- Consider these relaxation techniques

Instead of concentrating on falling asleep, concentrate on relaxing. Relaxation strategies that can help you sleep include controlled breathing, mindfulness meditation, progressive muscle relaxation, and guided imagery.

- If you can't sleep, get up

You want to prevent creating a mental link between your bed and your frustration at not being able to sleep. This means that if you've been in bed for roughly 20 minutes and still haven't fallen asleep, get out of bed and do something calming in low light. During this phase, avoid monitoring the time. Before going back to bed, try to divert your attention away from sleep for at least a few minutes.

- Experiment with various methods

Sleeping disorders can be complicated, and what works for one person may not work for another. As a result, it makes sense to experiment with various techniques to see what works best for you. Just keep in mind that new approaches can take some time to take effect, so allow your modifications some time to kick in before concluding that they aren't working for you.

- Keep a sleep journal

A daily sleep journal will help you keep track of how well you sleep and uncover elements that may be beneficial or detrimental to your sleep. For example, if you're experimenting with a new sleep schedule or other sleep hygiene modifications, keeping a sleep journal might help you track how well it's going.

- Consult a Doctor

A physician is the best person to give specific counsel to people who are having trouble sleeping. Consult your doctor if you notice that your sleep issues are worsening, persisting over time, harming your health and safety (for example, from excessive daytime sleepiness), or occur in conjunction with other unexplained health problems.

Healthy physical activity

Would you like to feel better, have more strength, and even add years to your life? Just get some workout. Regular exercise and physical activity have several health benefits that are difficult to overlook. In addition, exercise is beneficial to everyone, regardless of age, gender, or physical ability.

Distribute your activities over the course of the week. If you wish to lose weight, achieve specific fitness goals, or reap additional advantages, you may need to increase your moderate aerobic activity to 5 hours or more per week.

Before beginning a new physical activity, consult your doctor, especially if you have any worries about your fitness, haven't exercised in a long time, or have chronic health conditions such as diabetes, heart disease, or arthritis.

Benefits of physical activity

Do you need more persuasion to get started? Then, check out these seven ways exercise can make you happy and healthier.

1. It helps you lose weight

Exercising can help you avoid gaining weight or keep it off. This is because physical activity causes calories to be burned. The higher the intensity of the exercise, the more calories you burn.

Regular gym visits are fantastic but don't panic if you can't find a significant amount of time to work out every day. Any level of activity is preferable to none at all. To gain the benefits of exercise, simply become more active throughout the day – take the stairs instead of the elevator, or increase the intensity of your home tasks. The importance of consistency cannot be overstated.

2. It helps to combat health issues

Are you concerned about heart disease? Do you want to lower your blood pressure? Being active increases high-density lipoprotein (HDL) cholesterol, the "good" cholesterol, and decreases harmful triglycerides, regardless of your current weight. This two-pronged attack maintains your blood flowing properly, lowering your risk of cardiovascular disease.

Regular exercise can help prevent or manage a variety of health issues and concerns, including:

- Metabolic syndrome
- High blood pressure
- Stroke
- Arthritis
- Diabetes (type 2)
- Anxiety
- Depression
- Many types of cancer

It can also help with cognitive function and reduce the chance of death from other causes.

3. Exercise boosts mood

Do you require an emotional boost? Or do you need to let off some steam after a long day? A workout at the gym or a brisk walk can assist. Physical activity causes numerous brain chemicals to be released, making you feel happier, more relaxed, and less nervous.

When you exercise consistently, you may feel better about your look and yourself, which can raise your confidence and self-esteem.

4. It increases energy

Tired of supermarket shopping or housework? Regular physical activity can help you gain muscle strength and endurance. In addition, exercise helps your cardiovascular system perform more efficiently by delivering oxygen and nutrients to your tissues. And when your heart and lung health improves, you will have more energy to complete daily tasks.

5. It helps you sleep better

Having trouble falling asleep? Exercising regularly can help you fall asleep faster, sleep better, and sleep deeper. Just make sure you don't work out too close to bedtime, or you'll be too energized to sleep.

6. It revitalizes your sexual life

Do you think you're too weary or out of shape to enjoy physical intimacy? Regular exercise can improve your energy levels and promote your confidence in your physical attractiveness, both of which can help your sex life.

However, there's more to it than that. Women's arousal may be increased by regular physical activity. Guys who exercise consistently are less likely to experience erectile dysfunction than men who do not exercise.

7. It could be fun!

Exercise and physical activity can be entertaining. They allow you to enjoy the outdoors, relax, or simply indulge in activities that make you happy. Physical activity can also help you connect with family or friends in a social situation that is enjoyable.

So go hiking, take a dance class, or join a soccer team. Find a physical activity that you enjoy and do it. Are you bored? Try something new or do something fun with your friends or family.

Find motivation to exercise

You are not alone if you are having difficulty starting or sticking to a fitness routine. Despite our best efforts, many of us struggle to break out of our sedentary habits.

You are now well aware that there are numerous benefits to exercising, ranging from increased energy, improved sleep, and overall better health to decreased stress and anxiety. Furthermore, detailed exercise directions and workout routines are only a click away. But if understanding how and why to exercise was all that was required, we'd all be in shape. Making exercise a habit necessitates a change in your attitude as well as a strategic plan.

While practical issues such as a hectic schedule or poor health can make exercise more difficult, the most significant hurdles are mental for the majority of us. Perhaps it is a lack of self-confidence that prevents you from taking positive moves, or perhaps your motivation rapidly fades, or you become easily disheartened and give up. Unfortunately, we've all been like that at some point in our lives.

Whatever your age or fitness level, or even if you've never trained before, there are measures you can take to make exercise less daunting and painful and more pleasant and intuitive.

- Get rid of the all-or-nothing mentality
You don't need to spend long hours in a gym or push yourself to undertake boring or unpleasant things you despise to reap the

physical and mental advantages of exercise. On the contrary, a little exercise is preferable to none. In fact, even small quantities of physical activity added to your weekly routine can have a significant impact on your mental and emotional health.

- Be kind to yourself

According to research, self-compassion increases the chances of success in any given attempt. So, don't criticize yourself for your body, your current level of fitness, or your alleged lack of willpower. That will only serve to demotivate you. Instead, see your past mistakes and bad decisions as opportunities to learn and improve.

- Check your goals

You didn't get out of shape in a day, and you're not going to transform your body overnight either. Excessive expectations are the inevitable premise for rapid disappointment. Try not to get disheartened by what you can't do or how far you have to travel to obtain your fitness objectives. Instead of stressing on outcomes, concentrate on consistency. While mood and energy levels may improve rapidly, the physical payback will take some time.

Busting excuses for not exercising

Are you looking for excuses to avoid physical activity? There are solutions to each problem, whether it is a lack of energy or time or dread of going to the gym.

#1 - "I hate working out"

Solution: Many of us share the same sentiment. If pounding a treadmill or sweating in a gym isn't your idea of a good time, try to find an activity you enjoy, such as dancing, or combine physical activity with something more pleasurable. Take a walk around a gorgeous park at lunchtime, for example, or walk laps of an air-conditioned mall while window shopping, or walk, run, or bike with a friend while listening to music.

#2 - "I've no time"

Solution: Even the busiest of us may find time in our days for meaningful things. It is up to you to make exercise a priority. And don't think that a whole hour is required for a solid workout. Short 5-, 10-, or 15-minute bursts of activity can be quite helpful, as can cramming all of your exercises into a handful of weekend sessions. If you realize that you too busy during the week, get up and move around on the weekends when you have more time.

#3 – "I'm too weary"

Solution: Although it may appear paradoxical, regular exercise is a potent pick-me-up that actually reduces exhaustion and increases energy levels in the long run. Regular exercise will leave you feeling invigorated, rejuvenated, and attentive at all times.

#4 – "I'm out of shape / old"

Solution: It is never too late to begin improving your strength and physical fitness, even if you are a senior citizen or a self-proclaimed couch potato who has never exercised before. Exercise is rarely ruled out due to health or weight issues, so see your doctor about a safe regimen.

#5 – "Training is too hard"

Solution: The adage "no pain, no gain" is out of date when it comes to exercising. Exercising should not be harmful. And you don't have to push yourself until you're drenched in sweat or every muscle in your body aches to see results. Swimming, walking, or even playing golf, gardening, or cleaning the house might help you gain strength and fitness.

#6 – "I am not good at exercising"

Solution: Do you still experience physical education nightmares? You don't have to be athletic or well-coordinated to get in shape. Instead, concentrate on simple strategies to increase your activity level, such as walking, swimming, or doing extra housework. Anything that gets you moving will be effective.

Starting out carefully

If you've never exercised before, or if you haven't done sports or other exercises in a long time, keep the following health considerations in mind:

Health worries?

First, obtain medical approval. Before beginning to exercise, consult your doctor if you have any health problems, such as limited mobility, heart disease, asthma, diabetes, or high blood pressure.

Preparation is essential

Warm-up with dynamic stretching, which means vigorous movements that warm and stretch the muscles you'll be using as if it were a slower, easier version of the upcoming activity. For example, if you're going to run, walk first. Alternatively, if you're lifting weights, start with a few light reps.

Cooling down

It is critical to wait a few minutes after your workout to cool down and enable your heart rate to return to its resting range. After a run, for example, a brief jog or stroll, or some mild stretches after strength training, can also help reduce discomfort and injuries.

Drink a lot of water

Your body must always be adequately hydrated to function at its best. Failure to drink enough water when exerting oneself for an extended amount of time can be deadly, especially in hot weather.

Pay attention to your body

Stop working out if you experience any pain or discomfort! If you feel better after a brief rest, you can restart your workout slowly and carefully. But don't try to push yourself through pain. That's a formula for disaster.

Developing exercise habits

There's a reason why so many New Year's resolutions to get in shape fail before February. And it's not just that you don't have what it takes. Science demonstrates that there is a correct technique to develop habits that last. To make exercise one of them, follow these instructions.

Begin small and gradually increase your workout

A target of 30 minutes of exercise per day, five times per week, may sound reasonable. But how likely is it that you will follow through? The higher your ambition, the more likely you are to fail, feel horrible about it, and give up. It is preferable to begin with simple workout goals that you are sure you can attain. As you meet them, you will gain self-assurance and momentum. Then you can progress to more difficult objectives.

Use triggers to make it automatic

When it comes to creating an exercise habit, triggers are one of the secrets to success. In fact, studies suggest that the most dedicated exercisers rely on them. Triggers are merely reminders—a time of day, a specific location, or a cue—that cause an automatic reaction. They set your routine on autopilot, so you don't have to think about it or make any decisions. The alarm goes off, and you rush out the door to go for a stroll. You leave work early and go directly to the gym. You find your sneakers right next to the bed, and you're out and running. Find methods to incorporate them into your daily routine to make exercise a no-brainer.

Take care of yourself

People who exercise regularly do so because it provides them with benefits such as more energy, better sleep, and a greater sense of well-being. However, these are typically long-term advantages. Therefore, when you first begin an exercise program, it is critical to provide yourself immediate rewards for completing a workout or reaching a new fitness goal. Choose something you enjoy but won't allow yourself to do until after you've exercised. It can be as simple as drinking a cup of coffee or taking a hot bath.

Select activities that make you feel confident

You're unlikely to persist with an exercise if it's uncomfortable or makes you feel clumsy or inept. Don't choose activities like weight lifting at the gym or simply running because you think it's what you should do. Instead, choose activities that are appropriate for your lifestyle, physical abilities, preferences and goals.

How to make exercise more enjoyable

As previously said, a workout routine that is enjoyable and satisfying is much more likely to be maintained. On the other hand, no amount of willpower will keep you going with a workout you despise for the long haul.

Not just the gym

Is the notion of going to the gym making you nervous? It's ok if you find the gym inconvenient, pricey, scary, or plain dull. There are numerous alternatives to weight rooms and aerobic equipment for workouts.

Simply getting outside can make all the difference for many people. Even if you despise treadmills, you might enjoy running outside, where you may enjoy alone time and nature. Almost everyone can discover a physical activity that they enjoy. However, you may need to consider activities other than running, swimming, and biking. Here are a few activities you might enjoy:

- hiking
- horseback riding
- rock climbing
- ballroom dancing
- kayaking
- rollerblading
- martial arts
- paddle boarding
- Zumba
- fencing

Turn it into a game

Activity-based video games can be a great way to get started moving. Standing up and playing the so-called "exergames," such as skateboarding, dancing, or tennis, can burn at least as many calories as walking on a treadmill, if not far more. Once you've gained confidence, try stepping away from the TV and playing the actual thing outside. Alternatively, utilize a smartphone app to keep your workouts exciting and fun—some immerse you in interactive stories to keep you motivated, such as sprinting from zombie hordes!

Combine it with something you like

Consider your favorite activities and how you might include them in your fitness program. For example, watch TV while riding a stationary bike, talk to a friend while walking, take photos on a scenic trek, stroll the golf course instead of utilizing a cart, or dance to music while doing housework.

Make it more social

Physical activity can be a great way to socialize with friends, and doing out with others can help you stay motivated. A jogging club, water aerobics, or dance class may be ideal for folks who appreciate company but despise competition. Others may discover that a little healthy rivalry keeps the training interesting and pleasant. You may look for tennis partners, join an adult soccer league, find a regular pickup basketball game, or sign up for a volleyball team.

Consider using a mindfulness approach

When exercising, in order to avoid zoning out or getting distracted, try to focus on your body. By paying close attention to how your body feels as you exercise—the rhythm of your breathing, the way your feet strike the ground, the way your muscles flex as you move, even how you feel on the inside—you will not only improve your physical condition faster, but you will also interrupt the flow of worries or negative thoughts running through your head, easing stress and anxiety. Running, walking (particularly on sand), swimming, rock climbing, weight training, skiing, or dancing are all excellent ways to practice mindfulness.

Keep motivation to exercise

No matter how much you appreciate a fitness regimen, you may find that you lose interest in it after a while. This is the moment to spice things up and try something new or to change the way you approach the activities that have worked in the past.

Combine your workout with a sweet reward

While on the treadmill or stationary cycle, you can, for example, listen to an audiobook or watch your favorite TV show.

<u>Keep a record of your activities</u>

Maintain a log of your exercise and fitness improvements. Writing things down or using an app to log them, promotes dedication and makes you accountable to your routine. Plus that, it will be energizing to look back at where you started later on.

<u>Use the power of the community to your advantage</u>

You can join a variety of online fitness communities. Having others root for us and encouraging us through the ups and downs of exercise helps keep our motivation high. You can also try working out with pals in person or remotely via fitness apps that allow you to track and compare your progress.

<u>Find inspiration</u>

Read a health and fitness magazine or go to an exercise website to get motivated by individuals' photographs. Reading about and viewing photographs of healthy and fit photographs might sometimes stimulate you to exercise your body.

Is there also a spiritual wealth?

In the spirit of respecting all religions and those who do not believe in God and acknowledging that this is as abstract as hell, let us begin with some questions. What is your technique for dealing with and controlling your emotions and feelings? What do you do to live in the current moment while planning your future? Do you go to church? Do you practice meditation? Do you combine the two?

Awareness, in my opinion, is the truest definition of spiritual wealth.

How much in tune are you with your money beliefs? How much aware are you of why you make certain choices and decisions? How aware are you of what motivates your desire for the financial, social, time, and physical richness you wish to enjoy – and pass down to future generations? How conscious are you of what distracts you from focusing on each type of wealth individually?

I also believe that we need to rethink how we talk about wealth and our definition of it. As I mentioned in the first pages of this book, there is no single path to follow regarding wealth. And, just as I believe, we need to stop equating being rich with being wealthy for our individual and communal financial and emotional well-being.

So, let's make sure that when we talk about wealth, it is a multifaceted conversation rather than a one-dimensional one.

Chapter Six

REDESIGN YOUR LIFESTYLE

When Tim Ferriss' book "The 4-Hour Workweek" became a best-seller in 2007, it seemed like the buzzword "lifestyle design" sprang out of nowhere. Instead, it was a catchphrase, and as often happens in these cases, its original meaning faded rapidly.

However, more than a decade later, Americans require the concept of lifestyle design more than ever before. According to recognized data, we can state that Americans now work almost 8 percent more hours than they did 40 years ago, yet real incomes are lower today than they were in the 1970s.

It's far too simple to drift along with the current of life rather than steering your ship. However, if you do not define and build your ideal life, you will end up living your parents' vision, your boss's vision, your partner's vision, "the Joneses'" vision – everyone else's view of what your life should look like except your own.

People who create their ideal lifestyles are frequently referred to as "lucky." In fact, the people who fall into their occupations, families, and locations by chance are the ones who require luck. Without it, they are forced to live whatever lives come their way, which may or may not match their values and priorities.

Lifestyle designers do not require good fortune. Instead, they require foresight, perseverance, and patience. Regain control of your lifestyle by focusing on what is most important to you. To do otherwise is to live your life based on the priorities of others rather than your own.

What does lifestyle design mean?

In a nutshell, lifestyle design is intentionality. You define your ideal life, and then you make it a reality. If it sounds easy, it is – but it is far from simple.

I spent most of my life working hard to achieve my goals, often without thinking enough before making my choices. Instead, I followed the tide, even if every decision seemed to be an exercise in free choice at the time. A few years ago, I made a clean break with this situation; I quit my job, moved overseas, and radically changed my life all in the span of a year. I forewent a six-figure salary to pursue the unknown, which was not only frightening but also unpopular with everyone who knows me.

When my friends back home see my Facebook images from safaris or scuba diving, they say things like, "You're so lucky." With my full-time job, I can't do that." But it has nothing to do with chance. I forewent the consistent paycheck, 401(k), and paid time off that they were accustomed to. I renounced security and office camaraderie. In exchange, I can work from anywhere, set my own hours, and travel to ten different countries each year. However, I still make less than I did as a financial advisor working 12 hours a day for a multinational company.

Making sacrifices to create your ideal life is necessary. Most individuals, however, are unaware that they are already making sacrifices, whether they recognize it or not. The goal of lifestyle design is to ensure that you are sacrificing what is less important to you in order to prioritize what is most important to you.

Life on the laptop

Some people mix up lifestyle design and a mobile "laptop lifestyle." Unfortunately, the terms are not interchangeable.

I know people who have purposefully chosen to live a completely sedentary lifestyle. They have a regular in-person job and own a house. But everything about their work, home, and family life was well planned. Others create a mobile lifestyle, working from their laptops from anywhere on the planet. I used to be one of them.

Flexibility and the opportunity to work from anywhere are common topics in lifestyle design circles. The mobile lifestyle can be rewarding for those who are willing to take the risk. Nothing beats touring the world or relocating to another country to push your boundaries and stimulating growth. However, you can create a more traditional lifestyle by earning money in whatever way suits you best. You have control over everything from a full-time W2 job to freelancing and creating your own Internet business. It all depends on what you want out of life.

Budgeting & lifestyle design

One often-overlooked advantage of lifestyle design is that it may be used as a substitute for budgeting – a fantastic reward for anyone who despises spreadsheets and the math involved with budgeting.

You don't have to watch every dime to save money if you simply design your life to be low-cost. For example, when my wife and I moved abroad, we designed our lives so that we could live totally on the proceeds of an investment we made together. She teaches English online, and with that, we pay for our food and a few little extras. In addition, we purposefully chose a housing unit that does not require a car to get to work or amenities.

That frees us up to spend our money on entertainment and travel without affecting the money we invested and represents our financial security for the future. Of course, if we run out of money with five days remaining in the month, we'll have to get creative with what we've got in the cupboard. But that isn't usually the case since we know what kind of lifestyle we can live on the money we earn.

Set a high savings rate, then look for ways to automate your savings and other necessary costs. Take a holistic approach to create a happy life within your financial limits, and then settle into it. If you design it well enough, you will no longer need to budget; your savings and bills will take care of themselves.

After much thought, I determined that my top priorities were flexibility, travel, and independence. In return, I gave up security and stability. You can't have it all; therefore, it's up to you to select what you're willing to give up and what you're willing to accept in exchange. It's time to claim back control of your life, from your job to your finances to your personal life. And you can do it all while living on a smaller budget.

Key points of lifestyle design

Start by organizing your priorities in these four areas as you begin to plan your ideal life.

<u>Working style</u>

While your job is not the same as your lifestyle, it certainly constrains your lifestyle. Some jobs govern every other aspect of your life. For example, if you want to work as a police officer, you can expect to work when and how they assign you; you won't be able to choose your hours.

Pursuing a dream career may necessitate relocating to a different city, state, or nation. That's acceptable if you want to prioritize your profession over other aspirations on purpose or if your dream job puts you exactly where you want to be. However, meeting a partner may be challenging if your desired career takes you to the North Pole!

Consider these aspects to help you define and identify the proper job route, but keep in mind that your work is merely the starting point for your lifestyle choices, not the end. And it is never too late to change careers till the day you die.

Relocating?

Do you have a clear idea of where you wish to live? If your top objective is to live in a given location, you will almost certainly be able to do so, but it will almost always come at a cost. Unless you telecommute, your job possibilities may be limited. If you're single and want to meet someone, your dating options may be limited according to where you live. Similarly, the local cost of living may result in exorbitantly high housing costs.

Far too many people never consider if they should relocate. Even if they consider leaving their hometown, their perspective is restricted to the same state or country. Few people realize that they may live a luxurious lifestyle in some nations on $2,000 a month. Nowadays, distances are drastically reduced by new technological possibilities. Don't limit yourself when choosing where to live and consider the pros and cons of each solution.

Working routine

How many hours a week do you want to work? Which days, and what hours?

Working as a bartender entails working nights and weekends. Working as a litigation attorney implies working when the courts are open — and often for many hours after that. Some occupations allow for flexible working hours. As a hybrid entrepreneur and freelancer, I get to choose my hours, but it comes at the expense of employee benefits and stability. Again, it depends on your priorities and how much you're willing to give up in exchange for more freedom.

Personal relationships

Whether to marry, have children, or stay at home with your children should all be conscious decisions made in advance. They have an impact on your profession, wealth, and every other aspect of your life. They may necessitate other compromises, which is why you must prioritize them when you create your lifestyle, just as you do the other areas mentioned above.

How to design your ideal life

Prioritization is where lifestyle design begins and ends. You can achieve any life goal you want, but not for free; thus, creating your life entails surrendering lower goals to prioritize higher ones.

<u>Step 1: Identify and prioritize your goals</u>

First, list your top five priorities for a perfect existence. Consider the following:

• Where would you want to live if you didn't have any constraints?

• How much freedom do you desire in terms of working from home and setting your hours?

• What kind of work do you aspire to undertake the most?

• Do you want to get married?

• Do you wish to start a family?

• What is the importance of money to you?

• When do you want to become financially independent and retire?

• Do you have debts that you'd like to pay off?

• How many hours a week do you want to work?

• What are your personal interests, and how much time do you wish to devote to them each week?

Don't worry about getting it just correct at first; just start writing. For the time being, you merely want to get the ideas flowing. It becomes easy after you open the tap and your priorities appear on the page. Then you can pause, take stock, and begin sorting them in order of significance.

Step 2: Create an action plan based on *your* priorities

Once you've determined your priorities, the rest is a matter of execution.

If a specific career path is your top priority, then search the world for open employment. Don't stop networking and looking for jobs until you find one that fulfills your requirements, even if it's not in your current city, state, or country.

If living on the beach in Thailand is your first goal, check into ways to make money remotely, such as telecommuting or becoming a freelancer. By the way, that's what I did!

Whatever your priorities are, keep in mind that they come at a cost. A job that allows you to work from home and set your own hours may not pay as well. On the other hand, the high-paying work that sends you to oil rigs in Texas's wilderness may make it tough to meet potential singles or maintain a social life.

Create an action plan based on your top priorities. Some goals will complement one another; for example, paying off consumer debt improves your finances and acts as a suitable starting point for early retirement. However, you will inevitably give up something you desire to prioritize your top goals.

Step 3: Make all decisions based on your priorities

When faced with a difficult decision, including tradeoffs, use a simple litmus test to determine which tradeoff is lower on your priority list.

Remember that your priority list is a living, breathing thing. Your priority to pay off your debts vanishes the instant you do so. After working for a year or two, the dream job you valued over marriage, children, and geography may not be what you hoped for. Despite the high income, you may conclude that high-octane work isn't worth it because it takes away your nights, weekends, love relationship, and health.

You must maintain your finger on the pulse of your definition of a "perfect life." It would be best if you also considered whether each option reflects your priorities. Otherwise, you risk falling back into autopilot mode.

As you make more money, take extra care to avoid lifestyle inflation. Spend your excess money on your financial priorities rather than keeping up with the Joneses.

Work-life balance

Finding a balance among all forms of wealth requires achieving financial independence. This is a long-term goal that requires planning and commitment. However, it is right to find a work-life balance during the years it takes to reach this goal.

Work frequently takes precedence over all other aspects of our existence. Unfortunately, the ambition to achieve professional results often leads people to neglect other equally important aspects of their lives. Developing a positive work-life balance, on the other hand, is vital not only for your emotional, mental and physical well-being but also for your career.

In a nutshell, work-life balance is a condition of equilibrium in which a person prioritizes the needs of one's career and the needs of one's personal life equally. Some of the most common causes of a poor work-life balance are:

- Increased workplace commitments

REDESIGN YOUR LIFESTYLE   137

- More working hours
- Increased domestic obligations
- Becoming a parent

A strong work-life balance offers multiple benefits, including less stress, a stronger sense of well-being, and a lower chance of burnout. This benefits both employees and employers.

Employers who are devoted to offering work-life balance conditions for their employees can save money, have fewer incidents of absenteeism, and have a more loyal and productive staff. In addition, employers who provide choices such as telecommuting or flexible work schedules can assist employees in achieving a better work-life balance.

Consider the best method to create balance at work and in your personal life while developing a timetable that works for you. Work-life balance is less about splitting your day's hours evenly between work and personal life and more about having the flexibility to get things done in your professional life while still having time and energy to enjoy your personal life. For example, there may be days when you work long hours so that you can enjoy other activities later in the week.

Here are eight strategies for improving work-life balance, as well as how to be a helpful manager.

Recognize that there is no such thing as a "perfect" work-life balance

When you hear the phrase "work-life balance," you probably envision having a very productive day at work and then departing early to spend the rest of the day with friends and family. While this appears to be the ideal situation, it is not always attainable.

Strive for a realistic schedule rather than a perfect one. Some days, you may be more focused on work, while others, you may have more time and energy to pursue hobbies or spend time with loved ones. Balance is attained over time, and it does not happen overnight.

It's critical to stay fluid and always analyze where you are in relation to your goals and priorities. Of course, your children may need you at times, and you may need to travel for work at other times, but allowing yourself to be open to redirecting and analyzing your needs on any given day is critical to finding balance.

Find a career you enjoy

Although employment is a societal expectation, your career should not be stifling. Simply said, if you despise what you do, you will not be happy. Of course, you don't have to enjoy every aspect of your job, but it should be interesting enough that you don't dread getting out of bed in the morning.

Choose a career that you are so enthusiastic about that you would do it for free. If your job drains you and you find it impossible to accomplish the things you enjoy outside of work, something is wrong. You could be working in a toxic atmosphere, for a toxic person, or doing a job you don't like. If this is the case, it is time to look for other employment.

Make your health a top priority

Your primary priority should be your total physical, emotional, and mental wellbeing. If you suffer from anxiety or depression and believe therapy would help you, make time for it, even if it means leaving work early or skipping your nightly spin class. If you have a chronic condition, do not be afraid to call in sick on bad days. Overworking yourself hinders you from improving and may force you to take more days off in the future.

Putting your health first and foremost will make you a better person as well as a better employee. You will miss less work, and you will be happier and more productive when you are there. Prioritizing your health does not have to entail radical or drastic measures. It could be anything as basic as regular meditation or exercise.

Don't be frightened to unplug your devices

Cutting ties with the outside world on occasion allows us to recover from the weekly stress and creates space for new thoughts and ideas to develop. Unplugging can be as simple as taking a walk instead of reading work emails.

For example, reading a good book while traveling for work is a great way to disconnect from professional concerns and replenish your energy. With this strategy, you'll do so with greater motivation and clarity of thought when you return to your work.

Go on a vacation

Sometimes genuinely disconnecting requires taking a vacation and turning off all work for some time. Whether your vacation is a one-day staycation or a two-week trip to Hawaii, taking time off to physically and psychologically refresh is essential.

According to recent research, 52 percent of American employees had unused vacation days at the end of the year. Employees are frequently concerned that taking time off would interrupt the workflow and result in a backlog of work when they return. However, this apprehension should not prevent you from taking a much-needed holiday.

There is no nobility in failing to take well-deserved time off from work; the benefits of taking a day off far exceed the drawbacks. With careful planning, you may take time away without worrying about burdening your coworkers or returning to a massive workload.

Make time for yourself and your family

While your job is undoubtedly important, it should not take up all of your time. Before assuming this role, you were a person, and you should emphasize the interests or hobbies that bring you joy.

If you don't make a definite schedule for personal time, you'll never have time to do other things outside of work. Regardless of how absurd your schedule is, you ultimately have control over your time and life.

Make a calendar for romantic and family dates when organizing time with your loved ones. Planning one-on-one time with someone you live with may seem strange, but it will ensure that you spend meaningful time with them without work-life conflict. Of course, work keeps you busy, but that doesn't mean you should overlook your personal relationships.

Establish boundaries

To avoid burnout, set boundaries for yourself and your colleagues. For example, avoid thinking about impending projects or responding to work emails as you leave the office. Consider using a different computer or phone for work so that you may turn it off when you leave. If it isn't practicable, use different browsers, emails, or filters for business and personal platforms.

Whether you work from home or away from home, it is critical to define when you will work and when you will stop working; otherwise, you may find yourself responding to work-related emails late at night or on weekends off.

You can avoid it by informing your colleagues of any boundaries beyond which you would be unavailable due to personal obligations. This will help ensure that they understand and respect your workplace's boundaries and standards.

Establish goals and priorities (and stick to them)

Take note of when you are most productive at work and reserve that time for your most critical job-related activities. Avoid checking your emails and phone every few minutes, as they are huge time-wasters that derail your focus and productivity. Organizing your day can help you be more productive at work, which means you'll have more free time to unwind outside of work.

The simple living mindset shift

Over the past few years of simplifying and rebalancing my lifestyle, I've realized that there seems to be a pattern of thinking among people who choose to achieve financial freedom through minimalism.

It is simple to begin with noble intentions of simplifying life, decreasing clutter, or lowering commitments, but without the underlying shift in personal motivation and habits, it may be a tough lifestyle to keep in our culture that tells us the contrary, that more is better.

Simple living has become even more helpful, joyful, and sustainable as I have accepted these patterns of believing in the context of simplicity and converted them into habits I can act on. Continue reading to find out if you've already formed these habits or if you'd like to do so to reap the rewards they provide.

#1

First, accept imperfection! To be effective, simplicity does not have to be perfect; in fact, there is no such thing as perfection in life.

Simple life means different things to various people, and it will lead you along your own route and to your own goal. So don't compare yourself to other people's interpretations of minimalism or simplicity; instead, embrace yourself as you are, flaws and all, and keep going forward.

#2

Keep your focus on the present moment. Enjoying today, this present, the five minutes you spend washing the dishes, transporting the kids to school, or folding laundry, is a good habit to develop.

Nobody can guarantee the future, and as you start to appreciate the current moment, regardless of what you are doing or feeling, your thankfulness and appreciation for life, in general, will grow. This is not to say that you should not plan for the future, but rather that you should make the most of the present.

#3

Recognize that consuming and owning does not lead to happiness. Unfortunately, today's culture tells us the contrary message through TV advertising, celebrities, relatives, and even the 'keeping up with the Joneses' mindset in our communities.

Take a step back and consider what possessions truly are. They are typically products that make life easier but do not give happiness. Even sentimental items do not bring actual happiness; they may bring back memories, and the memories may make you joyful, but the object itself does not bring actual happiness. Recognizing this and making it a habit to purchase products with the goal of making life simpler will help lessen the need to acquire the latest technology or keep up with your friends' new gadgets.

#4

Consider making the world a better place for the current and future generations. This mental change enables us to form behaviors that will benefit us now and benefit others after we are gone. Reaching out to others appears to be one of the trademark practices of those who advocate simple living ideas, and this naturally extends to wanting the world to be a better place because you were a part of it.

For me, that means reusing stuff and purchasing recycled clothing, paper, and any other goods I can find that do not require new resources or cost the world or us. It also implies that I will say hello to strangers more frequently and will step outside of my comfort zone to assist and connect with people.

#5

Be aware that continuing to chase money is a limitation. Money does nothing to add to happiness if fundamental needs are addressed. We are taught that if we only had more money, we would be able to travel more frequently, be more generous, and give more experiences to our children. We could buy a nicer house, a fancier automobile, or any number of nicer "things."

When you look closely at this train of thought, you'll notice that we're attempting to buy happiness, which is simply not feasible. There will always be more to buy, therefore learning to be content with what you have and understanding the limitations of money to offer happiness is an important cognitive habit to establish.

#6

How much time do we devote to taking care of our possessions? Whether it's dusting off books, learning how to utilize our latest electronic gear, or doing five loads of laundry, ownership takes time, and time equals life. Reducing the number of goods you own gives you more flexibility and reduces stress.

Free yourself from the effort spent arranging everything in the garage, as well as the guilt you feel every time you see the treadmill you paid a lot of money for but never use. Get rid of things that take up your time and efforts yet aren't proving to be useful. It's ok to accept that purchasing something was a mistake, but don't compound that error by retaining it.

#7

Make the well-being of individuals you care about a top concern. This habit appears to spontaneously emerge as you establish the other mental habits mentioned above. Reducing physical and emotional clutter allows you to focus on what is truly essential, which for most of us is those we care about.

Making those we care about a priority should be, in fact, a priority, whether spending more time conversing at dinner with your husband or children, calling a loved one, or taking the dog for an evening stroll. However, just because something should be a certain way does not imply it is, so take the time to foster this train of thought by simplifying other aspects of your life to make room for it.

How to achieve financial freedom through minimalism

Whatever your definition of financial freedom is, adopting a minimalist lifestyle can help you get there. Simple living and minimalism assist you in prioritizing and discovering what you truly desire in life for some good reasons.

<u>Again, needs and wants</u>

As we learned in the second chapter, you soon learn how to distinguish between need and want when you simplify your life. We can define "need" as a requirement for survival and a "want" as a strong desire.

Now, I would suggest that you may also require something for mental or bodily comfort. For example, while you may not require more than one pair of shoes for survival, having a pair of athletic shoes and a pair of sandals is likely for comfort. Similarly, though you may not require family photos, having them nearby can be emotionally soothing.

Separating your wants and needs isn't about punishing yourself for having to live with less but rather about prioritizing. Do you need a discounted candle the next time you go shopping? Do you require a magazine? Do you require a large bag of potato chips?

We frequently say things like, "I need a vacation" or "I need to get my hair colored." But, at the end of the day, humans are remarkably resilient. We genuinely require very little to be comfortable, happy and fulfilled.

Minimalist living allows you to distinguish between what you genuinely need and what you simply want. When you stop spending money on needs, desires, needs, or frivolities, you suddenly realize you have more money than you thought!

<u>Simple living is ... simple!</u>

Simplicity is at the heart of minimalist life. Because you have fewer obligations, your schedule gets simpler, your need for technology gets simpler, and your time becomes more abundant. In addition, when you adopt minimalism, you feel less stressed and less like you are part of the so-called rat race.

When I took the decision to start simplifying my life, I was amazed at how quickly my priorities transformed. I no longer felt compelled to expend all of my energy to gain more money so that I could buy more things.

Simple, nourishing meals are usually less expensive than eating out. Weeknights become a lot less busy if you plan your meals for the week ahead of time and prepare them on the weekends. Even better, they're less expensive because you're less likely to give up and go out to eat.

Likewise, when you simplify your clothing, you only need the pieces that correspond to your capsule wardrobe or goal. As a result, you can mix and match your clothes, and you don't succumb to every fad or bargain. This allows you to save money on apparel and other costs.

Getting back to the basics of budgeting

Finally, minimalist living helps you to focus on what is truly important. Your behaviors become more focused and intentional. It's quality time when you spend it with others. When you buy something, it is because it meets a basic need.

The same is true for your finances. Simplify your finances as you simplify your life. Account for your monthly bills, save money, plan your debt repayment strategy, and move forward.

Begin by creating a basic budget. Consider the following:

- Mortgage/Lease
- Utility bills
- Monthly expenses (food, fuel, leisure, etc.)
- Insurance
- Savings

These are your standard "basic expenses." Then, consider what extra spending you might cut and redirect toward debt repayment. Is it possible to cancel any subscriptions? Do you require multiple movie streaming services? How about your (infrequently used) gym membership? When you pare down your budget to the essentials, your finances become simpler, and you get closer to the sensation of financial freedom.

Live within one's means

Many people in today's world are perfectly content to live beyond their means. This includes living in a more expensive place than they can afford, taking out car loans, purchasing technology, and spending money on things they don't need.

When you live a minimalist lifestyle, you are living within your means. Instead of being chaotic, your life becomes serene. Instead of seeking instant fulfillment, you ask yourself, "Is this really necessary?" Is it something I can afford? Is there another option?" Before you buy something new, use up what you already have.

We've gotten lousy at going without as a society. We all want our wishes to be granted right away (this is why many people are addicted to the instant gratification of ordering online). We anticipate that with the touch of a button, we will be able to obtain anything we desire in a matter of days, if not hours.

When you adopt a minimalist mentality, you begin to appreciate the worth of waiting and working for what you desire. When you put off making a purchase, it appears more precious and valuable. If you want to reduce your impulse purchases, even a short waiting interval will help you gain perspective.

Be resourceful

Do you know how to make minor repairs to extend the life of your belongings? Simple activities such as sewing on a button, mending a hem, or fixing a scratch can extend the life of your goods by years.

Learn basic repairs, sewing, mending, and other skills to help you save money and avoid buying new products. Often, you can locate gently used furniture for cheap or even free, and with a few repairs or a coat of paint, you can have a lovely piece for your house.

Similarly, you can locate amazing second-hand apparel that can be readily upcycled with minor changes. Before purchasing a new item for a particular occasion, check with friends to see if they have anything you may borrow. Check your local thrift stores if you can't find someone who has the item. You'll be shocked by the incredible items you'll find for pennies (but make sure you're only purchasing products that meet a necessity).

Learn how to cultivate your herbs, lettuce, and even fresh vegetables in a garden. By becoming more resourceful, you will be able to make the most of what you currently have and find creative ways to upcycle or thrift the products you require. In the long term, being resourceful will save you a lot of money and put you on the road to financial independence.

It takes up less space

People frequently want a larger home because they require more space to store their "things." Of course, you don't have to buy a smaller house, but learning to live a basic, minimalist lifestyle reduces your demand for square space.

After all, if you don't need space for an overflowing closet, overflowing cupboards, or knickknack shelves, you may live in a considerably smaller footprint.

Is my living space sufficient for my requirements (and the needs of my family)? Perhaps you'll discover that your living area is actually larger than you require. Cutting back on your rent or mortgage payment is a big step toward financial freedom. When you pare down your belongings, you may wish to sell furniture, collectibles, and other items to free up room and cash flow. Clean up your closets and tidy your kitchen cabinets. Look into what you could sell to make some extra money.

When you get rid of all the clutter in your home, it will feel bigger— maybe even too big! So it might be time to think about downsizing to a smaller space.

It helps you pay down your debts

Living a minimalist lifestyle will allow you to significantly reduce your debt. If you follow the basic budgeting rules, you should create and manage your monthly budget first. Then, look for wiggle room and use the extra to pay down your debts.

Fortunately, when you return to the fundamentals of minimalist living, you may discover that your simpler way of life frees up more income. When I streamlined my life, I was taken aback. I suddenly felt a lot less worried about money. I had additional money to put towards any debt since I only bought what I needed when I went shopping.

Before you begin working on debt repayment, you may find it helpful to put money aside for emergencies. Once you've saved up enough money for a rainy day, pay off your smallest loan first. Then, after you've paid off your initial loan, use the proceeds to your next smallest bill, and so on. This is known as the snowball method in budgeting.

Using this debt repayment technique is a rewarding way to achieve financial freedom. You'll notice your debt shrinking as you go, and it feels great to pay things off completely!

<u>Take a step back and look at the bigger picture</u>

When you simplify your life, you take a step back and evaluate. What is most important to you? What gives you a sense of meaning and fulfillment? What exactly do you require?

You study the wider image in front of you when you answer these questions. Suddenly, the quick fix of buying an impulse item in the checkout line or shopping for discounted stuff you don't need doesn't seem so appealing. These purchases aren't advancing you toward your larger goal.

It's astonishing how much simplicity frees me up to consider the larger ideas I have for myself and my family. For example, I've learned the importance of spending time together as a family, traveling as a family, and spending quality time outside. With these "larger picture" goals in mind, I prioritize and use our money to bring us there.

Most people think that financial freedom implies not worrying about money, which keeps you up at night and adds to your stress. Instead, it entails having enough money to spend time with loved ones, travel, and enrich your life with new experiences.

Living a minimalist lifestyle allows you to maximize your life because you aren't burdened by things that don't really matter. Instead, you are only concerned with purchases and behaviors that bring you joy, fill your needs, and move you closer to your larger goals.

Effective saving strategies

The indispensable premise of any path towards financial freedom and a better balance between the various types of wealth is to increase one's ability to save. If we learn to save money, we can, on the one hand, get used to living more simply, and on the other hand, increase the volume of our investments more quickly.

There are countless ways, strategies, and sets of rules that can assist you in reaching your financial objectives. However, all of the alternatives may be daunting – you may not even know where to begin. But, don't worry, we've got you covered. According to my counseling experience, the following are five of the simplest but most successful money-saving tactics.

Register your expenses

Undoubtedly, that's the first rule. If you want to reduce expenses and increase savings, first, you must understand where your money is going. Online budgeting tools, like Mint or BudgetPulse, make it simple to keep track of your expenditure.

Having a visual representation of your financial situation can act as a powerful in-the-moment gut check when you're asking yourself questions like, 'Can I afford it?' or 'Will this purchase move me closer to or further away from my goals?'

When you can see all of your purchases in one location, it's much easier to assess your financial situation. You can also see how your previous selections have led you to where you are now. For example, you may believe you eat out too frequently, but seeing how much money you spend on restaurants each month can be a motivating eye-opener. We can also use it in the future to track our progress when we begin to practice positive financial habits, such as growing savings and paying down debt.

Use the snowball method to pay off debt

If your goal for this year is to finally get out of debt, you're already on the right track – when you pay off your debt, you free up money for other financial goals. There are two main debt-reduction strategies: pay off your highest-interest loans first, or pay off your lower balances first. While the former makes more mathematical sense, research after research demonstrates that prioritizing your smallest balances, often known as the "snowball strategy," is the most beneficial.

List your debts in order of balance, start with the least sum and make minimum payments on all remaining bills. Once your smallest balance debt is paid off, use the money you were throwing at it to pay off the next lowest bill while making minimum payments on the others, and so on until you reach debt freedom. When you pay off a debt, you feel inspired and powerful, which gives you the motivation to keep going. And, according to the data, people who use the snowball method are more likely to stick to their debt-payoff targets.

You have to pay attention to one thing, though. The strategy works best when the interest rates on a consumer's debt accounts are identical. For example, assume one of your debts has a slightly higher balance but a significantly higher interest rate. In that instance, it makes more sense to concentrate on the higher-interest-rate debt. Be logical in your approach to debt, but keep in mind that personal finance is psychological, and quick financial victories can be a powerful tool.

Pay yourself first

First and foremost, pay yourself. This is the concept of always taking a portion of your paycheck and putting it aside before spending it on other things. It is simple to implement because it can be automated. Every payday, set up an automatic transfer from your checking to your savings account. Even if it's only $20 per paycheck, chances are you won't miss it, but you'll be pleasantly pleased with how much money you save over time. The PYF approach also assures that you don't have an "extra month left at the end of the money."

We've all been there: you get paid, go out to eat sushi, purchase that new top you've been eyeing, and go to the movies, only to find you won't be able to pay your auto insurance bill this month. You don't have this difficulty if you pay yourself first. Most bill providers offer automated bill pay, and you may frequently specify which day of the month you want that to be paid. Because your automobile insurance bill has already been paid, your discretionary funds are limited. In general, the goal is to ensure that your spending priorities are met before you have the opportunity to spend that money on less important things (no offense to sushi).

Set your goal of 10 percent saving rate

If you're unsure how much you should save each month, try for the 10% rule of thumb. If you consistently save 10% of your salary, no matter how much you make, you will always have the assurance that you are living within your means.

It's a ballpark figure, so don't feel guilty if you don't exactly meet it. Set a target of 10%. And if you discover that you wish to save even more money, you can always change this proportion later. This rule works well when combined with the Pay Yourself First technique. Set up automated bank transfers for the beginning of each month if this sounds too tough. Money set aside for savings is transferred from your checking account to your savings account before it may be spent on something else. Consider saving 10% as a strategy to empower yourself to make consistent contributions to your financial health year after year.

Try the "no-spend month" challenge

Money challenges are enjoyable because they make excellent financial habits a game. Start your savings campaign off right with a no-spend month. It's easy: Commit to spending only on basics for 30 days. Instead of driving, walk or bike everywhere, bring your lunch to work every day, and take advantage of free entertainment choices such as exploring local parks. And if you make a mistake, don't be disheartened. The goal is zero, but the overarching goal is to just spend less and save some money.

The activity can also help you reconsider several of your expenditures and spend more wisely in the future. You will not only save a lot of money over this one month, but you may also find yourself reevaluating past spending patterns and deciding you prefer your own inventive, low-cost options. Thus, this practice can have a significant impact on your balance sheet.

CONCLUSION

The world has changed, and it's continuously changing. Some of the most deeply rooted beliefs, the result of centuries of consolidation, are faltering or have already completely collapsed.

I ask you only a seemingly simple question: would you like to have more money or more time?

Until a few years ago, a question like this would have seemed meaningless if not downright provocative.

Millennials are playing by new rules that reflect fundamental economic changes. If time is our chief commodity, then we want it as much as possible – and that means outsourcing things to get more.

In the past, people saved money; now, we desire to save time.

This book shows how wealth is a much broader concept than we might instinctively think. We learned to distinguish, within the concept of wealth, four different aspects, all equally important.

The first is the most obvious, financial wealth. The pressure to accumulate money is omnipresent in our culture, and it can have a negative impact on your ability to develop other forms of wealth. According to what we have learned, money must become a tool to help us live the life we want, not a goal itself. Therefore, focus on the strategies I described to earn and invest as much as possible in the most efficient way.

Your social wealth, or personal connection in society, is the second sort of wealth. This is decided by your relationships with others, such as family, friends, and the community. Because humans are social and emotional beings, accumulating social wealth is essential. Someone who is socially wealthy can rely on others to meet their emotional requirements.

Time wealth is the freedom to choose how, with whom and where you spend your time. Working more to earn more money takes away your social wealth by not allowing you to enjoy your time with people you love or even pursue your passions in life. You can't cultivate those ties, and the bonds weaken. Since you are overworked than ever, also your time wealth suffers. That's why only those who understand time is a finite resource aim to become financially independent.

When you actively look after and improve your physical and mental health, you have health wealth. This can be accomplished by exercise, a good diet, and managing stress, worry, and other mental pressures. This improves your general happiness and well-being. Everything is interconnected. Poor mental health makes money management more difficult, and anxiety over money leads to bad mental health. Improving your health wealth is all about developing good habits and living a balanced lifestyle.

Now is the time to take advantage of all that you have learned on these pages. Your goal should be to constantly work to improve your life in all kinds of wealth. Don't allow society or your job to draw you to pursue only financial or social wealth. Time and health wealth are equally important.

Since I've been down this road before, I can assure you that with study and commitment, you can achieve the perfect balance of wealth and enjoy life 100%!

Have a great journey!

www.ingramcontent.com/pod-product-compliance
Lightning Source LLC
LaVergne TN
LVHW020932170825
818860LV00030B/1020